HERE LIES BILLY THE KID

HERE LIES BILLY THE KID

BY DAVID S. TURK

COLD WEST PUBLISHING

An imprint of Creative Texts Publishers, LLC
Barto, PA

TABLE OF CONTENTS

AUTHOR'S NOTE

In 2011, Sunstone Press published my book *Blackwater Draw*, which highlighted the results of a case study of three murders in Blackwater Canyon. Popularly seen on the screen in "Young Guns II," William "Buck" Morton, Frank Baker, and William McCloskey were killed by Billy the Kid and his Regulators. In doing so, I wanted to add something new to the catalog "chock full" of Billy the Kid tomes. I did not consider *Blackwater Draw* controversial, and the work added to the existing body of research. Still, the book saw publication at the end of a controversial period for anyone writing about the Kid. Despite soldiering through these years, I eventually turned to other writing projects.

It is with much hesitation I decided to write *Here Lies Billy the Kid*. Unlike my other "Kid book," this short history is frankly revealed. While *Blackwater Draw* focused on a few Regulators, *Here Lies Billy the Kid* aims directly at the Kid's final resting place and its connection to one Regulator. The sensitivity is obvious. In the recent past, discussion of these events lacked the necessary historical objectivity. Through this study, some hard truths are brought to light, and some long unanswered questions are settled. Without a dual investigative study of the Bowdre family alongside that of the Telfer hearing, this would have been impossible to complete.

I want to note something important from the onset. This is not a "hero" and "villain" account. If there is any blame to be assessed, there is only that of overreach and human error. I found hard feeling, oversight, and rash action, but no inference drawn to anything more than that. However, my research findings located flaws in the official record caused by these same human oversights. In interviews with members of either side in the dispute over moving the body of Billy the Kid, I felt they were all honorable people and there is no attempt to state otherwise here.

Secondly, I do not question where the body of the Kid actually is or should be buried. As a historian, my job is to present the facts so the reader makes an individual judgment. My own personal views are primarily traditional, yet open-minded, of the Kid's burial location. In addition, I only offer weight to "Brushy Bill" or other alternative theories in this study where they intersect with the main theme of the work. The presence of William Morrison, who accompanied "Brushy Bill" and co-authored *Alias Billy the Kid*, figured in this account in a related fashion. Therefore, "Brushy Bill" is a brief sidelight in this history. Morrison himself is more of a key figure.

Finally, there is the importance of the grave itself. The missing wooden marker and the subsequent problems surrounding that event have been recounted. Thanks in large part to the memories of Jack Potter and members of the Bacon family, more information surfaced on the New England Live Stock Company. The old cemetery at Fort Sumner saw its share of flooding. It was vital to recount all the trials this parcel of land went through. At the same time, outsiders weighed in on the Billy the Kid legend, and sometimes this did not sit well.

Although still a sensitive subject, *Here Lies Billy the Kid* corrects pieces of the historical record. I know that any physical search for the Kid, Charlie Bowdre, and Tom O'Folliard in the Old Fort Cemetery would be too arduous to undertake in today's environment. That does not mean the question should not be asked or addressed at all. The story of the outlaw's burial is just as much about Lincoln as it is about Fort Sumner. Modern tourism and community pride has made the spirit of Billy the Kid more important than the physical body today, and he still rides everywhere in American nostalgia.

David S. Turk
December 2018

ACKNOWLEDGMENTS

This work may be small in size, but the account is comprehensive, powerful and intricate. The research, writing and editing took a number of years to complete, many between other writing projects. In any comprehensive work of this kind, there are numerous people and institutions to thank in the wake of completion. For the sake of space, I will keep it brief.

The first "thank you" goes to my family for the time and patience allowed for research and writing the manuscript. There was a necessary series of research ventures to Arkansas, Mississippi, New York, Oklahoma, New Mexico, and Texas to obtain vital primary source information on both Charlie Bowdre and the 1961-62 hearings to move Billy the Kid's body. The support of my family made the discoveries possible.

My extended family made this equally helpful. Steve Sederwall is one of the most innovative people working in Old West history during modern times. His use of investigative techniques and police instinct, combined with the collaboration with historians and specialists, was a ground-breaking practice when the Billy the Kid case was re-opened in Lincoln County, New Mexico in 2003. He took a lot of heat, as did the two former sheriffs who filed with him, for using techniques that were not widely understood or used before in that way. I did understand him, because I lived in that world already. If you look at the studies conducted today, the investigative methodology is mainstream and not "crackpot science." Whether people like it or not, Steve Sederwall raised that banner. In the course of this, he and I became close friends—like brothers in fact. His wife Carolyn, daughter and son-in-law Brett and Nina McInnes, and their daughter Ashlyn—have been a second family to me and opened their home to me in New Mexico for my many stays. I miss those in that family that are gone--particularly Lonnie Littman, Walter Dollahon, and faithful canine companion Kate.

Other friends I'd like to thank connected to this work are Sallie Chisum Robert, Bob Alexander, Cliff Caldwell, and Retired U.S. Marshal John L. Moore. His wife is a former Fort Sumner resident. There are many more I have not named.

I'd also like to thank the many individuals who assisted me in my research. Again, they are too numerous to completely mention here, but include Betty and John Grabbe, John Lemay and the friendly folks at the Southeastern New Mexico Historical Society; Phil Scott; Sue Tennell; Debbie White; Myrl Jane Humphrey; Nellie Ruth Jones; Joe Salazar; Sharon and Eugene Degner; the late Johnson Stearns; Harold and Mike Stewart; and the late Lloyd Davis.

Many institutions went out of their way for me. Special mention is made for the following: The University of Arizona Special Collections; University of New Mexico, Center for New Mexico History; University of Texas, Briscoe Center for American History; University of Texas at El Paso, Special Collections; Haley Memorial Library & History Center, Midland, Texas; National Archives & Records Administration; New Mexico State Archives & Records Center; Library of Congress' Manuscript Room; De Baca and Lincoln County Courthouses; Brigham Young University, L. Tom Perry Special Collections; Denver Public Library; and Palace of the Governors, Fray Angelico Chavez History Collections Library.

Lastly, thanks to Dan Edwards and Cold West Publishing for keeping the faith in this powerful little book!

DT
January 6, 2019

INTRODUCTION

There are too many books about Billy the Kid. They are written on every conceivable angle of the outlaw's brief life, psyche, and unending legacy. The cultural saturation of this icon, whether perceived as a hero or a villain, never peaked. National interest in the long dead gunslinger ebbs and flows. Once a new discovery or historical wrinkle is corrected from the often-errant early biographies of his life, it seemed five or six new books appeared on the market. It proved one thing. The study of the life and death of Billy the Kid is a historical phenomenon that never ends.

At the center of the excitement are two New Mexico villages associated with the long-dead outlaw: Fort Sumner and Lincoln. They could not be more different. Most of Billy's life was spent in Lincoln County, but he was a notable presence in Fort Sumner. By most accounts he died and lay buried in its borders. Both towns served as social centers while the Kid was alive, although modern times brought economic hardship to both. Kid-associated tourism generated dollars, but the two villages diverged on their methodologies. By the 1950s, Lincoln tried to recreate itself as a "Williamsburg of the West," while Fort Sumner preferred basic strategies around the grave. After all, the grave is what visitors usually came to see.

In 1961, Lois Telfer, a red-headed beautician supposedly related to Billy the Kid, upset the balance between the two communities. Although Lincoln County could have done so on its own, her presence bolstered a representative group's desire to bring back the Kid's remains for reburial. This group of like-minded "movers and shakers," which then included a pivotal figure named William Vincent Morrison, raised the possibility for the return of the body.

Officials in the Fort Sumner area angrily disagreed. The result appeared more like a typical lawsuit or hearing. Officials and boosters of the two counties ripped at each other's historic pride. In the process, good people rushed to judgement, made critical legal errors, and one even died before it was resolved.

The key to the Telfer hearing and its associations with the grave of Billy the Kid lay beyond the outlaw himself. Rather, it was his old friend Charlie Bowdre. It was around this compadre's life and remains that Telfer's opponents based their hearing strategy. Therefore, it was necessary to study Bowdre's life and family as closely as the Kid's. Often misunderstood in life, Charlie Bowdre's presence was again felt in the De Baca County Courthouse in 1961 and early 1962.

Although this account appears a cross between a courtroom drama and a soap opera, the 1961-62 Telfer hearing and its associations with the grave of the Kid were serious business. It was not always about money, but civic pride. Perhaps the reason many historians avoided this episode in the Billy the Kid lexicon was due to its "newness." A few of the participants may still be alive, although enough time has elapsed for historical perspective. However, the real reason for any focused study in modern times is the lack of interest for western historians. It remains an untapped book to add to the genre, and perhaps one of the last original topics on Billy the Kid.

CHAPTER ONE

BURIAL ARRANGEMENTS

Two and one-half miles east of Fort Sumner on U.S. Highway 60, and six miles south on a graveled-all-weather country road is the grave of Billy the Kid... In a little unkept cemetery, dotted with crosses of many unknown graves, Billy the Kid lies in company with his two pals, Tom O'folliard, and Charley Bowdre, who were killed a short time before Billy the Kid met his death, at the hands of Sheriff Pat Garrett, who was also responsible for the deaths of both O'folliard and Bowdre.[1]

These were the words of J. Vernon Smithson, who worked with the Works Progress Administration in April 1936. His descriptive entry of Billy the Kid's grave at Fort Sumner New Mexico seemed explanatory and plain. However, it belied the real controversy. 25 years later, an unexpected battle arose between officials in two county jurisdictions. In effect, the controversy began on July 14, 1881 with the burial.

Enterprising citizens of Fort Sumner have erected a monument marking the graves of Billy the Kid, Tom O'folliard, and Charley Bowdre. The three were buried side-by-side... Lawless they might have been, they sleep in peace in this dreamy little cemetery where nothing disturbs the quiet, but the soft gurgle of water in the nearby ditches and the cooing of doves to their mate. In such surroundings, it is easy for the imagination to conjure back the days of Old Fort Sumner and Billy the Kid.[2]

The article appeared an imaginary setting. In 1936, Fort Sumner was a former military outpost that quietly developed into private residences and ranches. Several miles from the town center was the remains of the old military post and cemetery. Entering the town limits, Fort Sumner, the highway greets visitors with a billboard that highlighted their locale as Billy the Kid's "final resting place." Until recent times, there were two museums to complement the cemetery. Local citizens discussed their famous (or infamous) occupant— depending on their individual viewpoint.

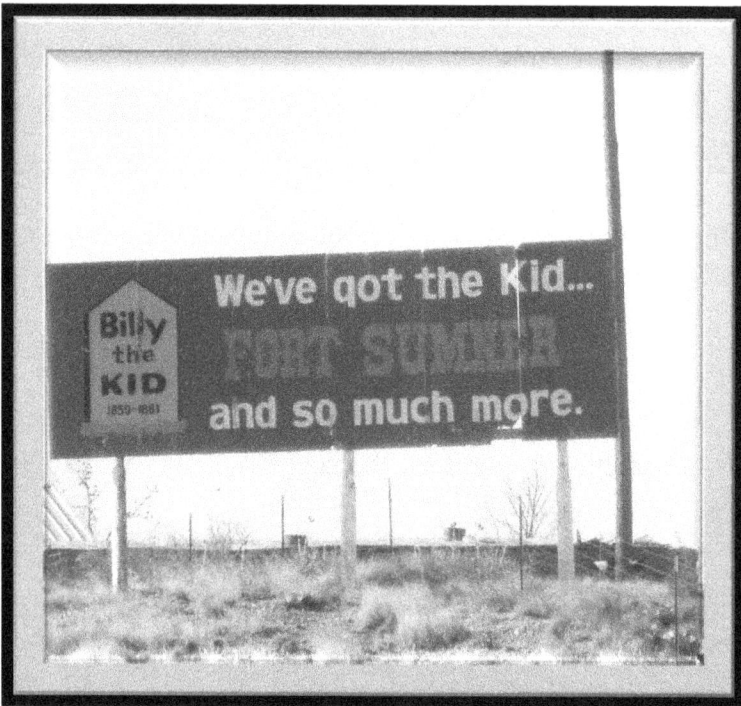

A Billboard Greets Visitors to Ft. Sumner, New Mexico, ca. 2005.
Author's Collection.

Over the years, a fierce loyalty emerged several times in opposition to those who disturbed the Kid's noted resting place. The location of the cemetery, down a winding road with few stones or markers, boasted walled borders. A bygone flood removed some of the markers, but the most noticeable feature of the cemetery is a stone memorial encased in a cage. On the memorial are engraved the names of three men: William Bonney, Tom O'Folliard, and Charlie Bowdre.[3]

The stone memorial covered a conflict over the location of the graves in Fort Sumner. Part of the problem was the lack of primary material that surrounded the burial of Billy the Kid. The existing documentation included a controversial coroners' report, written in Spanish, and the personal accounts of several residents at the time. Also, the memorial was a modern addition erected in the mid-20th Century. The docent at the museum opined that the concrete sidewalk possibly covered the body of O'Folliard. In the corner of the cemetery, the stone markers denoted the graves of the Maxwell family. Peter Maxwell, in whose darkened bedroom Billy the Kid supposedly met his fate, lay in state. The mystery was not the grave, but the Kid's body.[4]

Within a very short time after the shooting, quite a number of the native people had gathered around, some of them bewailing the death of their friend, while several women pleaded for permission to take charge of the body, which we allowed them to do. They carried it across the yard to a carpenter shop, where it was laid out on the workbench, the women placing lighted candles around it according to their ideas of properly conducting a 'wake' for the dead.[5]

These were the words of John William Poe, one of Lincoln County Sheriff Pat Garrett's deputies during his term. He recounted the Kid's death long afterward, but important details were chronicled for posterity.

All that occurred after the Kid came into view in the yard, up to the time he was killed, happened in much less time than it takes to tell it, not more than thirty seconds intervening between the time I first saw him and the time he was shot. From Garrett's statement of what took place in the room after he entered, it appears he left his Winchester rifle standing by the side of the door, and approached the bed where Maxwell was sleeping, arousing him and sitting down on the edge of the bed near the head.[6]

From Poe's eye, Garrett was melancholy. He and the Kid knew each other a long time, and allies for a time. This changed little of the events in Pete Maxwell's bedroom on the night of July 14, 1881. In Poe's *The Death of Billy the Kid* (1933), he acknowledged there were many "wild and untrue stories" of the incident.[7] It was unclear whether Poe meant these were claims by some area citizens, or whether details were parsed from certain accounts. However, editors assisted future researchers by including the coroner's jury report in the book's epilogue.

To the Attorney of the First Judicial District of the Territory of New Mexico, Greeting:

This 15th day of July, A.D. 1881, I, the undersigned, Justice of the Peace of the Precinct above named, received information that there had been a death in Fort Sumner in said precinct and immediately on receiving the information I proceeded to the said place and named Milnor Rudolph, José Silva, Antonio Saavedra, Pedro Antonio Lucero, Lorenzo Jaramillo, and Sabal Gutierres a jury to investigate the matter, and, meeting in the house of Lucien B. Maxwell, the said jury proceeded to a room in said house where they found the body of William Bonney alias 'Kid' with a bullet wound in the chest on the left side of the chest, and, having examined the body, they examined the evidence of Pedro Maxwell, which evidence is as follows: 'As I was lying on my bed in my room about midnight on the

14th day of July, Patrick F. Garrett entered my room and sat down on the edge of my bed to talk with me. Soon after Garrett had seated himself William Bonney entered and approached my bed with a pistol in his hand and asked me, "Who is it? Who is it?" and then Patrick F. Garrett fired two shots at him, the said William Bonney, and the said Bonney fell upon one side of my fireplace, and I left the room. When I returned three or four minutes after the shots, the said Bonney was dead.' The jury has found the following verdict: 'We of the jury unanimously find that William Bonney was killed by a shot in the left breast, in the region of the heart, fired from a pistol in the hand of Patrick F. Garrett, and our verdict is that the act of the said Garrett was justifiable homicide, and we are unanimous in the opinion that the gratitude of the whole community is due to the said Garrett for his act and that he deserves to be rewarded.'

M. Rudolph
President

Anto Sabedra
Pedro Anto Lucero
Jose X Silba
Sabal X Gutierrez
Lorenso X Jaramillo

All which information I bring to your notice.
Alejandro Seguro
Justice of the Peace[8]

Poe's book featured both English and Spanish versions of the coroner's report, as edited by Colonel Fulton. Once the body was examined, the burial arrangements began. Unfortunately, little documentation exists to confirm more details. The Kid was already a household name, and more so upon his death. For a famous person, a curious lack of written documentation and first-hand source accounts left a vacuum of doubt.

An interesting account on the burial was written in Spanish by local resident Paco Anaya about 1930. The text was later compiled into book form and entitled *I Buried Billy* (1991). He was known as an honorable man in the community, so Anaya's account was a treasure when it appeared. His relatives provided the original manuscript to Texas publisher Jim Earle, and he included it as a volume in his early west series of history books. Anaya actually wrote his account five years after an author named Walter Noble Burns wrote *The Saga of Billy the Kid* (1926), which created a stir when published. He freely criticized Burns, but many other New Mexicans did the same. Burns ignited a flame bed of interest in the life and deeds of Billy the Kid, or rather renewed it. Various texts, including Pat Garrett's own *The Authentic Life of Billy the Kid,* had long been the bedrock of popular view. In addition, Burns was an outsider who conducted his own research. More of a generalist, he studied various Old West figures such as Wyatt Earp and Joaquin Murietta.[9]

Paco Anaya, who personally met Billy the Kid, was in a position to criticize Burns. More importantly, he gave important details of the burial. Pat Garrett gave Maxwell, according to Anaya, twenty-five dollars to "put good clothes" on the deceased man.[10] Maxwell diligently did so, "*bought a beige suit, shirt, and undershirt, shorts, and a pair of stockings. I, the writer, and my brother, Higinio Garcia, and several others of those that were there, dressed Billy with those clothes then we laid him on a high bed, one of those narrow ones, and we took him to the saloon where they held dances. There we watched, and on the next day we buried him.*"[11]

Although Anaya explained the Kid's entire career through his memories, his account explained the local citizen's participation in the burial process. The three citizens tasked were Anaya, Don Jesus Silva, and Charles Foor. Most descendants agreed that they buried Billy the Kid at Fort Sumner as described. *I Buried Billy* was published as a book, but portions utilized in an article "I Hid Out Billy the Kid," in a magazine entitled *Personal Adventure Stories*, published in October 1937. The documented account changed over time, probably as a result of faded memories.[12]

Pete Maxwell fashioned the wooden marker for the Kid's grave. He used a long wooden slat removed from the parade ground picket fence near his own house. A portion was cut off and hammered to fashion a cross upon the plank. The words "Billy the Kid, July 14, 1881," the customary memorial facts of the time, was inscribed. Some reported an additional phrase in Spanish. It was later taken and never recovered.[13]

The first publicized effort at removing Billy the Kid's body from Fort Sumner began in 1925. Frank Coe, a friend of Billy the Kid, was said to have visited Fort Sumner to make an inquiry into moving the body back to Lincoln County. According to his son Wilbur, Frank Coe felt it was too expensive an operation to attempt. The poor condition of roads made it even more difficult to transport. At the time, little fanfare was made of Coe's plan. However, this was prior to the popular books written on the Kid. The publication of Burns' *Saga* and a new addition of Garrett's history in 1927, edited by Fulton, changed the landscape of the legend. The Kid—and his corpse—became a treasured commodity.[14]

A slew of literary efforts followed and contributed to the argument over the legend of Billy the Kid. The combination of two books—Burns' *Saga* and Fulton's edition of Garrett's history—nationalized the conversation. There was a surging interest in locating research on the life and death of Billy the Kid. Some pointed to Burns, who had a broad readership after writing about other Old West personalities. However, Fulton was a thorough historian and researcher, and an entrusted and knowledgeable resource on the Lincoln County War.

According to Fulton, through information from cowboy and politician Jack Potter, in an early article called "the Grave of the Kid and Its Marker," Burns had assistance researching the marker. He recalled, *"Walter Noble Burns, I believe, took old Charley Foor down to Fort Sumner to locate the Kid's grave and to get a description of the marker and the inscription on the same. I can say that old Charley was almost right when he described it. The only mistake was when he said a bunch of soldiers came along a few years afterwards and shot it to hell. This part was a mistake."*[15]

Historian Robert Mullin, who regularly corresponded with Fulton for many years, noted that *"MGF [Fulton] was informed that part of the site of the old Military Cemetery was washed away by flood wateres [sic]."*[16] Mullin also noted the general confusion of locating the grave's actual location had further problems. Eve Ball, through a Fort Sumner resident, stated the cemetery was actually situated in a different location altogether. *"The location of the cemetery was changed in 1920 to higher ground. 'Pedro Analla and Jusus [sic] Silva were the only two pallbearers / Bonney funeral/ they could locate. They disagreed on the location of the Kid's grave; the sites each thought right were not very far apart, so they put the coffin ha[l]f-way between the two locations."*[17]

Although the arguments over exact location continued, popular culture found new avenues to the Kid through movies and serials. Jack Potter penned several articles in the early serial magazines from the 1930s. "The Kid's Friend Don," based on the horse of the deceased outlaw, was published in R*anch Romances* in October 1936. A second article, also published in R*anch Romances* in May 1937, was entitled "Post-Mortem on Billy the Kid." Only months after that, A. P. Anaya had his story "I Hid out Billy the Kid," in *Personal Adventure Stories*, in September 1937.[18]

New Mexico boosted its tourism in marketing both historical landmarks. Both Lincoln and Fort Sumner benefitted from the publicity that emanated from it. Both locations took advantage. In July 1930, Fort Sumner found a solution for the lack of a grave marker for the Kid. In an article entitled "City to Mark Grave of Billy the Kid," a permanent memorial was planned. It read in part, *"A concrete curbing has been placed around the graves and a concrete slab over the spot were Billy rests. In time, it is planned to erect a marker."*[19] As the wooden marker was missing, the plot was known by a handful of survivors with distant memories. Jesus Silva, 72 at the time of article and a member of the coroner's jury, was largely responsible for locating the plot.[20]

The one agreed-upon point among witnesses and historians is that all three men were buried together. Billy the Kid, Charlie Bowdre, and Tom Folliard were buried next or near each other. Aside from the flooding of the nearby Pecos River and other "Acts of God," the cemetery's relocation was problematic. The rumors the three bodies were dug up at the time were quelled through a flyer found in the archives of Historical Society for Southeast New Mexico in Roswell. Adelina Welborn, a member of the Maxwell family, rallied citizens to speak out against the sale of the cemetery to pay taxes on an irrigation ditch. She propounded on the "historical value" of the graveyard, which indicated the bodies were still there.[21]

The slew of media reports and Hollywood interest in filming the "Old West," including a number of films on Billy the Kid's life and career brought a new popularity in the 1930s and 40s. The renewed interest, particular on international levels, brought tourists to Lincoln and Fort Sumner. More historians studied the Lincoln

County War. However, the popularity came at a price. Until the late 1940s, there were few accounts or persons who disputed the initial accounts—particularly that of Garrett. The accounts of the Spanish populations were largely not widely known, but they ironically knew Billy the Kid more than most. The co-author of the Garrett book, Ashman Upson, was a former newspaper scribe who left a large number of unanswered questions and created a vacuum for inquiry.

There were some well-to-do people who both enshrined and eschewed the legend. In 1940, a letter from James Warner to Mrs. R.A. Doak gave some insight on a new marker, this one of stone.

I erected a stone for the grave of Billy the Kid in Fort Sumner a couple of weeks ago. The reason I did this is because his life has always been fascinating to me, from the time I was nine years old. When I recently read more of his life and knew that his grave was unmarked I decided to mark his grave, as I am in the Memorial business.[22]

James Warner made the "original" headstone, complete with carvings of crossed pistols, a row of bullets, and an inscription above that read "Truth and History." The letter reveals Warner as a fan but further contents of the letter reveals more.[23]

My personal interest arose when I was nine years old, as my uncle rode the range New Mexico in 1895 and he knew and told details of Billy the Kid and the man who knew him. He also knew the man, Pat Garrett, who killed him, very well. My uncle always regarded Pat Garrett a worse character than Billy the Kid ever was.[24]

With the marker of Billy the Kid in place, things appeared to be settled in New Mexico. Both Fort Sumner and Lincoln maintained twin legacies. Tourism continued to thrive for decades. Lincoln maintained its historic appearance, almost frozen in time. Fort Sumner, on the other hand, maintained its role as a county seat and group. It fostered a Museum dedicated to the history of the Kid, so both communities were invested. By the 1950s, new challenges appeared. These involved little about movement of the body in the grave, but whether the person in the grave was Billy the Kid at all.

CHAPTER TWO

THE TRAILS OF CHARLIE BOWDRE

Charlie Bowdre is the reason that the Fort Sumner grave mystery still exists. The Mississippi native came west to make his fortune, but ended up a dead man in December 1880. Despite his friend's end, much of the Kid's career was spent with Bowdre or in close proximity to him. In time, Charlie Bowdre proved the key to much of the controversy surrounding the burial.

Charlie was born in Wilkes County, Georgia in 1848. He was the oldest son of planter Albert Rees Bowdre and his wife Lucy Meriwether, a distant relation to the famed explorer Meriwether Lewis. The Bowdre family was prominent, and soon after his birth they relocated to the present village of Senobia in DeSoto County, Mississippi. An indenture from Charles S. Meriwether to Albert R. Bowdre, dated January 1859, revealed a survey of 543 acres. Although prosperous and hardworking, the Civil War interrupted their fortunes. Albert attained the rank of major in the Confederate forces, and several of his in-laws also served as soldiers. Lucy Bowdre died in January 1866 shortly after its conclusion.[25]

Charlie Bowdre was the oldest of eight children. Little is known of his youth or his relationship with his parents. His closest sibling was his brother Benjamin Thomas Bowdre. He was born in January 1857, one of a set of twin brothers and nearly a decade Charlie's junior. Benjamin's granddaughter, Betty Grabbe, noted few relatives spoke about Charlie Bowdre within the family after his departure. Most of his siblings married into local Mississippi families, but Charlie never fit in. He stayed in Mississippi until about 1872-73, but subsequently moved west in search of adventure or enterprise. The family did keep in touch for some time.[26]

One recipient of letters was Charlie's sister Eppie and her husband Donald McKay Dockery. Like his father-in-law Albert, Dockery was a prominent farmer. After his service in Confederate General Nathan B. Forrest's cavalry during the Civil War, the family settled in Hernando, Mississippi. Before the death of Major Bowdre in January 1880, the family scattered in different directions. Other than a small family cemetery at Senatobia, there are few traces of Charlie's early days.[27]

Charlie Bowdre was already in New Mexico Territory when Major Bowdre died. In 1873, the first mention of his presence appeared on a published "uncalled mail list" with Postmaster G.W. Bailey of Silver City, in the southwest portion of the territory. Billy the Kid's friend Frank Coe remembered that Bowdre *"came to New Mexico as a bookkeeper on a large ranch."*[28]

During this early period, Bowdre crossed paths with Josiah G. "Doc" Scurlock. According to Doc's great-grandsons, Harold and Mike Stewart, he was nicknamed "Doc" for his work in a charity hospital in New Orleans and alleged medical training at Tulane University. Supposedly Bowdre and Scurlock met in Arizona Territory while prospecting for gold. Doc was an Alabama native, and he shared regional ties to Charlie Bowdre's birthplace. In the summer of 1876, the two engaged in the ownership of a cheese factory on the Gila River. The Stewarts believed a youthful William Bonney came to work there for a short period. He was "looking for a handout" and a place to hide.[29]

The cheese factory was not to last. According to the Stewart brothers, the pair sold the business and ventured to Lincoln County to purchase land. This was a difficult achievement without the support of the "House," the power-brokers of the region. This group of politicians, lawyers, soldiers, and large landowners controlled and steered much of the territorial wealth. They were cool to outside interests of any kind. In Lincoln, their representatives were merchants James J. Dolan and Lawrence Murphy. The pair borrowed from Dolan and Murphy, but Mike Stewart revealed the cause of estrangement from them. *"They borrowed money from the Dolan Murphy [faction] to buy land...kind of swindled them to buy land that was already taken [public lands], so I think that's how they got crossways of them."*[30]

Despite their bumpy beginnings in Lincoln County, both Bowdre and Scurlock began an itinerant lifestyle. Historian Donald Cline found "Charley Bowdrey" [sic] on a voter registration listing dated November 3, 1876. Lincoln County's poll book identified him in the county's third precinct.[31] They worked as cowhands and buffalo hunters, and traveled widely within their domain. In the summer of 1877 Charlie Bowdre was observed in Dodge City, Kansas. Texas author Ed Bartholomew, in his book on outlaw Jesse Evans, noted Bowdre was in the buffalo-rich lands around Fort Griffin, Texas, but after the great slaughter of the herds.[32] He probably transported hides from there to Dodge. While there he met others who figured prominently in the forthcoming Lincoln County War. According to Bartholomew, he met Jesse Evans and some of his shady gang while in Texas, perhaps around Tascosa or Mobeetie.[33]

The well-traveled Bowdre was more recognizable than most of his contemporaries. Bartholomew's description of Charlie Bowdre was of good general reputation. Save for his association with William Bonney, who both he and Doc Scurlock worked with, most would not view him as a typical outlaw. Bartholomew wrote, *"[He] wore a scrawny sandy mustache, had a high forehead and usually wore a fine black hat, when flush. He was a stickler for the wearing of the vest, summer and winter. He was a good neatured [sic] sort of fellow, easy to get along with at times.* "[34]

There was one early occasion in which Charlie Bowdre was considered an aggressor. The Stewart brother's uncle, Joseph Buckbee, co-wrote an article with historians Philip J. Rasch and Karl Klein on Doc Scurlock for the English Westerners Society in 1963. The text recounted a skirmish that occurred on August 5, 1877 between drunken cowboys Bowdre and Frank Freeman and a number of unnamed Lincoln residents and visitors. After shooting an African American officer, wounding him, Freeman exhorted his companion Bowdre to lawyer Alexander McSween's home. They heard rancher John Chisum was there, and they called out to him while firing haphazardly into the residence. A servant returned fire, and the pair ran off.[35] The *Mesilla Independent* newspaper related the two *"fired forty shots in at the doors and windows doing no other damage than to furniture."*[36] Another recounting stated there was 20-50 shots, which *"broke doors and windows, hit sewing machine in house..."*[37] Although both Bowdre and Freeman received general acknowledgement, there were inconsistencies in the various accounts. A third man named "Armstrong" was said to have fired as well, and later killed by a pursuing posse. The same account related Freeman had pistol-whipped the officer, and that the gun accidentally fired.[38]

After the events in town, Lincoln County Sheriff William Brady and a posse went after the pair. News accounts placed them together with outlaw Jessie Evans and an outfit known as "the Boys." No doubt they were associates of Evans, but not members of his gang. In fact, they often were at odds. Brady's posse, supported by soldiers from nearby Fort Stanton, was on the move by August 14, 1877. They were not hard to find. At Bowdre's ranch, the groups engaged in a melee. Freeman fell dead in the withering exchange of gunfire, and Charlie Bowdre fled to the Ruidoso River. Their allies were shown little mercy either. Scurlock and George Coe were both arrested for possession of stolen horses. As they were not part of the pursuit, they were released.[39]

Bowdre and Scurlock received nothing but trouble from Jessie Evans. They travelled to Mesilla's Corn Exchange Hotel, where on September 22, 1877, three names appeared together on the register: Josiah G. Scurlock, Charles Bowdre, and Richard M. Brewer, all from "Ruidoso N.M."[40] Soon after, the three returned and sought Evans and his gang for the stolen horses and mules. They found them at Warren Shedd's San Augustin Ranch near the Organ Mountains. According to Rasch, Buckbee and Klein, negotiations failed and with the property's impressive defenses, a fight was pointless. On October 3, charges were filed against Bowdre and Scurlock. The lesser offenses were charged against Scurlock for "Disguising to Obstruct the Execution of Law" and "Carrying Deadly Weapons," while Bowdre carried two causes for murder. These actions, and the difficulties with Murphy and Dolan, forced the new ranchers into an alliance with others caught in a similar situation.[41]

Bowdre, Brewer, and Scurlock found a friend in newcomer John H. Tunstall, a British citizen who tried his hand at ranching. Like them, Tunstall ran afoul of the House. Along with Chisum and lawyer McSween, the small ranchers had some limited protection in their numbers. A number of cowhands worked for Tunstall— including their old employee William Bonney. Dolan and Murphy viewed the consolidation as opposition and a viable threat to their control of the region. An escalation of conflict between these two groups was inevitable.[42]

Violence broke out within months. The oft-told result of the escalation was the ambush and death of Tunstall on February 18,

1878. Bowdre and others were moving horses and livestock when a posse, augmented by Evans and a few of his ragged band, shot the Englishman when he separated from the group. His death particularly shook Bonney, as he considered Tunstall a close friend. He and his allies, led by Brewer, plotted their next move. After obtaining legal pretext, their posse--known as the "Regulators"-- combed the country in search of their enemies. Near Seven Rivers in the Pecos Valley, the band caught two of their quarry, William S. "Buck" Morton and his cohort Frank Baker. On the return journey they were joined by William McCloskey, a ranch-hand who worked for both sides in recent months. By way of Chisum's South Spring Ranch, the Regulators and their captives started for Lincoln to turn them over to Sheriff William Brady. Some in the group, particularly Bonney, felt their captives would never see prison. The band avoided pursuit and took an obscure sheep farming trail to Blackwater Canyon, a distance north of the Hondo River.[43]

While they stopped to water their horses in Blackwater Canyon, an opportunity to kill the captives arose. Although Brewer cautioned against this action, Bonney and some of the others proceeded. McCloskey attempted to interfere, and he was cut down. Morton and Baker knew they were next. They ran across the canyon floor, but fell dead in a hail of bullets after a short chase. Brewer was understandably miffed, and both Bowdre and Scurlock were caught in something they could not extricate themselves from. Brady and his allies would be after them.[44]

Perhaps they knew the gamble they took, because the Regulators struck Sheriff Brady first. On April 1, as he and several deputies rode through the town of Lincoln, they were prey to an ambush. Six of the Regulators, not including either Bowdre or Scurlock, hid behind a wall in wait for their adversary to come within range of their guns. Of the five in Brady's party, two died. Fire concentrated on the Sheriff, who was killed along with his deputy, George Hindman. The death of the lawman raised the stakes for all who allied with them.[45]

On April 4, 1878, Bowdre and his allies found a place to hide at Blazer's Mill, a trading post at the Mescalero Apache settlements. It was here that Charlie Bowdre committed his most serious crime, although the death of Andrew L. "Buckshot" Roberts was periodically wrongly attributed to the Kid. Almer N. Blazer was a youth at the time, playing with friends, when he saw the shady characters. He later recalled to a newspaper reporter that Roberts, visiting a friend, prepared to depart the area when he spied the Regulators dining nearby. However, this account was challenged by one of the Regulators. George Coe claimed Roberts was there to collect on a reward posted for them.[46]

Coe's comments on the Blazer Mill fight came during a public meeting in Mescalero, New Mexico on June 12, 1932. When introducing the topic, he noted that only Bowdre and Brewer were the mature adults in the encounter. Coe said,

The Kid was only about seventeen or eighteen years old; there wasn't but one or two men in there that was at maturity, that was Dick Brewer and Charlie Bowdre. Charlie Bowdre was an experienced man and he started to arrest that man [Roberts], and he was the only man we had that could have done it. He killed him, he didn't arrest him.[47]

Further, George Coe questioned the motives of "Buckshot" Roberts the day he was killed. Far from an innocent, the gunman had motive.

...this "Buckshot" Roberts he had just come into Lincoln just a day or two before this excitement, and he had stayed all night with my cousin. My cousin lived at Tinnie—where Tinnie is now. And he went up and got into the excitement, and then they started right off

to offering a hundred dollars reward for us, and that fellow is the very fellow that took the hundred dollars reward – "Dead or alive," said they had rather we were dead than alive, and that is the proposition he took.[48]

Coe explained that the group was not aware of a reward until informed by a friend. They camped out to avoid contact of nearby soldiers. They quietly crossed the Rinconada to the Blazer place. All manner of citizens visited Blazer's store, and the family stayed staunchly neutral. Nearly noon, the Regulators ordered dinner, but they established a guard to keep watch for pursuing soldiers. "Buckshot" Roberts was discovered on the property, and Dick Brewer did not want to take chances. Bowdre and Bonney both volunteered to arrest him. According to Coe, there was no actual intent to kill him.[49]

The confrontation began as a negotiation, but ended violently. George's cousin Frank Coe confronted Roberts in the doorway first, and he encouraged a peaceful surrender. However, Roberts refused—either by fear or motive. It hardly mattered after that. Charlie Bowdre led the arresting group, and said "throw up your hands." Roberts demurred with "not much," and exchanged fire. Both bullets hit their mark with different results. Roberts' bullet hit Bowdre in his belt buckle, bounced, and struck George Coe in the hand. Bowdre's bullet hit its mark, but "Buckshot" fired several more times and forced his would-be-captors back. Then matters worsened when he barricaded himself inside a saw mill.[50]

The conclusion of the firefight at the Blazer Mill had a high price. According to George Coe, Dick Brewer moved towards the building in hopes of looking inside. Roberts discerned the general direction of gunfire and returned fire. One of his bullets hit Brewer—some sources say squarely in the head. He died shortly after. Shortly after, a company of soldiers appeared and the Regulators slipped away. However, Bowdre's shot did its work. The mortally-wounded Roberts lived until the following morning. According to Blazer, *"It was very near noon when he died."*[51]

As the spring of 1878 turned into summer, there was another tie in the friendship between Charlie Bowdre and his friend Scurlock. Both men courted daughter of Spanish rancher Fernando de Herrera and his wife Juliana Martin. The fearsome, red-headed Fernando sired a dozen children and moved to the Ruidoso River Valley from the mountainous Basque region of Spain.[52] His proficiency with firearms was more than equal to his natural skill in ranching sheep. Doc was rightfully worried. Both Stewart brothers stated, *"Fernando was reported to be the best rifle shot in Lincoln County."*[53] Despite the real possibility of being a target for Fernando's rifle, Scurlock fell in love with his 15-year-old daughter Maria, known as Antonia. Not taking chances, the couple eloped. Antonia reportedly never saw her parents again. In due course, Charlie met her younger sister Manuela, six years younger than Antonia.[54]

Despite his wife's influence, Charlie Bowdre's reputation as an outlaw haunted him. Although his reputation as an "outlaw" was at times guilt by association with the Regulators, he exacerbated his own problems. The death of Andrew "Buckshot" Roberts at Blazer's Mill ensured Bowdre's status as an outlaw. Still, by most accounts, he was generally of good character.

For the greater part, Charlie Bowdre's family remained in Mississippi. His siblings kept in touch. He was close to two of them: his brother Benjamin Thomas, some 10 years his junior and a twin, and his sister Eppie Dockery. Like his older brother, Benjamin was prone to mischief in his youth. Granddaughter Betty Grabbe remembered the family considered the possibility of sending him to New Mexico Territory to live with Charlie.

Evidently, my grandfather, Benjamin Thomas Bowdre, became quite interested in a divorced woman, so the family was going to send him "out west" to Charlie, so that he could cool off a bit. Charlie wrote back and said it wasn't a good time to send him at that time, because things were getting bad in New Mexico.[55]

Apparently, the family received word of the outlawry. It complicated his relationships, and prevented Benjamin from joining Charlie. Instead, he moved to Plumerville, Arkansas, just northwest of Little Rock, and joined other members of the family.[56]

True enough, Charlie Bowdre experienced great difficulty in New Mexico Territory. Pursued by Brady's successors, they wrongly suspected him with the group of Regulators responsible for his death. A group of ranchers from the Pecos River Valley joined them. In the chaotic days that followed, Bowdre was reportedly captured by Jessie Evans near Brewer's old ranch. In turn, he was rescued by the Kid, who rode into Evans' camp and "bluffed" the mercenary into releasing his friend. Several of their contemporaries were not as lucky. Frank McNab, who was one of Brady's assassins, was cut down in an ambush, while Frank Coe was wounded and captured. New Lincoln County Sheriff John Copeland received military aid from the cavalry at Fort Stanton to round up Bowdre and some of the others in Lincoln.[57]

Bowdre and the others were released by mid-May. Cattleman John Riley complained that the Regulators stole a number of horses and killed a herdsman. According to Phil Rasch's research, Bowdre and Scurlock were accused of trying to sell stolen cattle, and the dubious source was James J. Dolan. Governor Samuel Axtell and lawyer Thomas Catron, both more prominent members of the "House," communicated to Colonel Edward Hatch that "Scurlock's party" stole from Catron's own herds. A greater error was that these reports mistakenly viewed Bowdre and Scurlock as the leaders of the Regulators. He was at most a nominal leader, but Bowdre probably deferred to Scurlock in most instances.[58]

The cat-and-mouse game with the "House" concluded in the summer of 1878. By July, they replaced Copeland with Deputy Sheriff George Peppin and indicted suspects for the murder of Roberts. Peppin was friendly to Dolan and the House, and he aggressively dogged the Regulators. On July 14, they appeared in Lincoln and tempers flared. Most were in lawyer Alexander McSween's house, but Bowdre was with a separate group inside the Isaac Ellis' House at the eastern end of town. Peppin initially bypassed them in favor of McSween, but they attempted to dislodge them five days later. By then, the McSween House was in flames and a number of occupants within dead, including the lawyer himself. Bowdre and Scurlock withdrew after a half-hearted fight. The "Five Days' Battle" was over.[59]

The aftermath proved enough bloodshed for both Charlie Bowdre and Doc Scurlock. After they stole horses from the Apaches, and killed an Indian Agent in the process, they outrode a pursuing contingent of soldiers. Once the military men returned to their quarters, the Regulators crept back to Lincoln. More opposition awaited them there, and it necessitated they "lay low." They participated in a few cattle and horse raids, but Bowdre and Scurlock left for Fort Sumner about September 1, 1878.[60]

At Fort Sumner, the pair found regular employment. Any interest in stolen livestock was sold to the other Regulators. Scurlock, and for a time Bowdre, worked for Pete Maxwell, the son of the late grant owner Lucien Maxwell. Through Maxwell and other local residents at nearby Sunnyside, the village near the installation, the Kid's friends had a base of support. Grocer and bar owner H.A. "Beaver" Smith had a popular stopover, and seemed to know everybody around. His boarders were Petra Valdez and her son Jose, an employee not yet 20 years old. The younger Valdez was an associate of both Bowdre and the Kid. He was also handy with the pen, and wrote fluently in both English and Spanish.[61]

The Kid's nemesis also appeared at Fort Sumner. Patrick F. Garrett was a 28-year-old former buffalo hunter and cowboy. Like Doc Scurlock, he was born in Alabama. His background resembled Bowdre's, but according to writer and bookseller Jeff Dykes, surpassed him in ambition. Garrett passed through Fort Griffin, Texas, where he met a number of cowhands that moved to New Mexico Territory. He "took a riding job" in the Pecos Valley in late 1878 or early 1879. He worked in different businesses around Fort Sumner, including a stint with Pete Maxwell.[62]

For a time, Charlie Bowdre and the Kid ran in different circles. While the Kid and most of the Regulators continued with their herd to the town of Tascosa, in the Panhandle of Texas, Bowdre and Scurlock stayed with their families in the Fort Sumner region. They met Thomas Griffin Yerby and Nasaria Leyba, his companion (and possibly wife), at a ranch east of Fort Sumner. Despite Virginia roots, the rancher prospered through his work with various western business firms. Historian Donald Lavash studied Yerby and his connections to the Kid and the Regulators. By 1872, Yerby worked for wholesalers Becker & Company near Albuquerque, then subsequently as a bookkeeper for Charles Ilfeld & Company in Las Vegas, New Mexico Territory. Yerby's success in the Ilfeld firm afforded him the land and the ranch house near Fort Sumner. He met Nasaria, then sixteen years old, as a potential housekeeper. Lavash found sketchy references to a marriage at Anton Chico, but the Federal Census of 1880 listed Nasaria as a boarder. Two children, Juan and Florentina, were born between 1876 and 1879. Both had Yerby's surname.[63]

During late 1878 or early 1879, Charlie Bowdre hired on as the ranch foreman for Thomas Yerby. Lavash's study reported that the Bowdres were likely married by this time. Nasaria and Manuela Bowdre were the same age, and the three spent much time together while Yerby worked for Ilfeld in Las Vegas. They spent weekends in town shopping and attending social functions. Billy the Kid appeared on occasion, particularly during the time he sought a pardon from the new governor, Lew Wallace. Rumors of romance between the Kid and Nasaria cropped up after the two were seen dancing together, and the birth of daughter Florentina brought hushed whispers that the child was not Thomas Yerby's. However, Lavash rejected this second rumor. If the rumor was true, Yerby would have fired Bowdre immediately.[64]

For a time, life at the Yerby Ranch settled down. After the Kid met with Governor Lew Wallace in March 1879, he drifted once again into Texas. Yerby stayed at the ranch more often. Bowdre continued on the job as ranch foreman, and among his cowhands was a young lad named Thomas Folliard, also known as O'Folliard. He was a former Regulator in Lincoln during the "Five Days" in July 1878. Another notable name was Tom Pickett, who was employed as a rider.[65]

The quiet times at Yerby's ranch ended for Charlie Bowdre. Doc Scurlock decided to leave for Vernon, Texas. According to Harold Stewart, he tried *"his best to take Charlie with him when split with the Kid and his gang."*[66] Scurlock left, but he never convinced Bowdre, who stayed at the ranch. In hindsight, Bowdre probably calculated better fortunes with most of the other former

Regulators in Tascosa, Texas, and his newfound connections through his work as foreman.

Scurlock's departure was a watershed moment in Charlie Bowdre's life. Without him, his decision-making was prone to influence from others. For his part, Scurlock drifted through Texas for the rest of his long life. He operated a stagecoach stop in Vernon, and later a confectionary shop. Notably, he wrote papers and theses for college students. Scurlock and his wife Antonia had eight surviving children, who he encouraged to read classic literature. He never discussed his experiences in New Mexico Territory in any detail. Doc passed away in Eastland, Texas at the age of 79 on July 25, 1929.[67]

The Kid eventually reappeared in New Mexico Territory. After a period of "laying low" as he drifted through the region, life in Tascosa lacked both excitement and opportunity. His love for gambling brought him to Las Vegas, where he brushed elbows with fugitive Jesse James. While there, he renewed his acquaintance with fellow cowhands Billy Wilson and "Dirty Dave" Rudabaugh. Both were suspected of criminal activity, but primarily theft. Eventually, the Kid also re-established his connections to Charlie Bowdre and visited him at the Yerby Ranch.[68]

The Kid used his connections to the Yerby Ranch. In addition to Charlie Bowdre, the two young cowhands O'Folliard and Pickett hid some of his stolen stock. They used a "temporary corral" on the property and on the nearby ranch of Manuel Brazil and Erastus Wilcox. After a time, they sold them across the territorial borders. According to local resident Charles Frederick Rudolph, the group's decision to utilize the ranch was to prey on John Chisum's nearby herds. Several of the herdsmen felt Chisum owed them payments from their previous employment with him. Rudolph referenced an entire cattle herd was once driven to the village of White Oaks for a quick sale. The same livestock sold to neighbors.[69]

On January 11, 1880, the Kid and some companions stopped at Milnor Rudolph's ranch near Sunnyside on their way to their new hideout. The preceding day, according to Rudolph, he killed a man in a Sunnyside drinking establishment. Young Jose Valdez was tending bar when a braggart named Joe Grant wandered in. Among his past taunts, Grant thought he could take on the Kid. Unbeknownst to him, his "quarry" was in the cantina. After Grant drank and slurred a number of insults, Rudolph wrote that Grant's bravado finally hit the Kid's nerves. Oddly, he complimented the inebriated man on his pistol. Given the chance to examine it, the Kid "emptied its chambers" of its ammunition.[70]

Other accounts of the Grant confrontation differ from Rudolph's version. Robert Mullin wrote that the two cowboys engaged in shooting bottles from a shelf in the bar. The Kid supposedly received an insult during the game, and he shot Grant while he drew a gun that either jammed or lacked bullets. Rudolph claimed Grant was the aggressor, drawing his empty gun first. Either way, the Kid shot him dead. It marked the end of a relatively peaceful period for him.[71]

With Billy the Kid back to his dangerous ways, Charlie Bowdre was in a fix. He dared not cross his old friend, but he was not interested in returning to the hard days of the Lincoln County War. As foreman of the Yerby ranch, his conscious bothered him. Although contact with his relatives in Mississippi was scarce, one definite contact was his brother-in-law, Donald McKay Dockery. The husband of his sister Eppie moved their family to the northern Mississippi town of Hernando.[72] One relative mentioned that *"the family did hear from Charlie after he left home, but after he got on the wrong side of the law, his name wasn't mentioned anymore."*[73]

Bowdre indeed found himself on the wrong side of the law. Despite his connections to community businessmen like Yerby and Joseph C. Lea, the Kid's new partners played a dangerous game. The Dedrick Brothers, who ran a number of businesses around Las Vegas and Lincoln County, fell in with a counterfeiting ring. While the rustling continued, and the Yerby ranch remained a cover for their stolen goods, the related operation was in a livery stable in the boom town of White Oaks. There, a number of characters with aliases appeared alongside the Kid and Billy Wilson. Before long, their counterfeit bank notes bought livestock, mining stock, and dry goods. Although the "funny money" looked real, merchants were alert. In addition, there were several high-profile robberies.[74]

The operation combined counterfeiting, robbery, and rustling, and payed off in the short term. One story related that Charlie Bowdre received a visit from Porter Stogden and his wife. Mrs. Bowdre was friends with Stogden's spouse Emily, and they visited at a critical moment. Father Stanley Crocchiola wrote of the meeting in his book *Desperadoes of New Mexico*.

Mrs. Stogden took to visiting Mrs. Bowdre and the two became very good friends. Charles Bowdre impressed her as a gentleman with his neat clothes and dark complexion. Mal Pais and White Oaks were beginning to make mining news. Mrs. Bowdre told Mrs. Stogden on her last visit that a man was killed somewhere along the road and two sacks of gold dust stolen from him. When she went home to get supper ready her husband was sitting at the table, two small sacks before him. He was tighter than a drum. He said he struck it rich. Of course, she believed him. She had no choice.[75]

Whether or not Bowdre actually struck it rich, the meeting coincided about the time the counterfeit notes surfaced in the region.

In or around August 3, 1880, Billy Wilson made the mistake of passing a fake bill in J.A. LaRue's store in Lincoln. This establishment was under control of a suspicious Jimmy Dolan. Another surfaced in Tularosa, which raised more attention. Dolan and others wrote the Treasury Department. Secret Service's Special Operative Azariah F. Wild was dispatched from their New Orleans office to investigate the activity. The organization followed other branches of the counterfeiting operation throughout the country, and strongly suspected New Mexico Territory was its newest outpost. In September Wild met with U.S. Attorney Sidney Barnes in Santa Fe. After he later conferred with Dolan, suspicion fell on Wilson and his "employer," the livery stable owned by the Dedricks in White Oaks. In addition, Wilson's travel to the Fort Sumner area was noticed.[76]

Wild knew the exchange of the counterfeit notes bought more than household goods and groceries. He distrusted the current sheriff, George Kimbrell, as friendly to some members of the suspected scheme. Instead, the agent appealed for assistance through Barnes, which proved a wise move. Wild tapped law enforcement resources without Kimbrell's direct involvement. Instead, he utilized local residents in the Fort Sumner area. One of the latter was Patrick F. Garrett. Once Wild organized his allies, he focused on his opposition. A man named West (at first he believed was named "James") appeared to be the guiding figure, but he also noted the flashy roles of both Wilson and the Kid. In his daily report of October 18, he mentioned others he believed involved, including Charlie Bowdre and Thomas O'Folliard.[77] In White Oaks, Wild found an informant and wrote, *"There were five men making counterfeit National Bank Notes in denominations of $50 and $100. Have nearly $200,000 made."*[78]

Through his informant, Wild and the Secret Service established an active branch of a large counterfeiting operation. The local informant, named "DeVours" in Wild's reports, described the inner workings of the ring. He is first mentioned by name in Wild's message of October 9, 1880, after an introduction from Edgar A. Walz in Lincoln. While the details assisted his efforts, the information was not always current or accurate. One of the "gang" the informant identified to Wild was Doc Scurlock, who had long departed for Texas. Unless Doc Scurlock returned for a visit, he had little to no involvement. Charlie Bowdre was tied to the scheme through his associations. The Kid and Billy Wilson were already implicated. Associates Thomas O'Folliard and Thomas Pickett were likewise drawn in. Through their frequent visits or employment at Yerby's ranch, suspicion naturally fell on Bowdre.[79]

On October 16, a robbery of the mails north of Fort Sumner left a large number of open envelopes and letters littered on the ground. Within three days, Wild learned the counterfeiting operation moved. It became apparent the motive behind the crime was informational. The robbery was an act of desperation as word of the investigation passed. In hindsight, the act proved a vital mistake made by the ring.[80]

By early November, Wild was ready to make arrests, and the need for multiple posses marked the rise of the Kid's associate Patrick F. Garrett as a law enforcement officer. He worked with experienced lawmen like Robert Olinger, but the sheer need for more help near Fort Sumner forced him to write Joseph C. Lea. Wild requested that Garrett take part in the posse. With Lea and Garrett in the fold, coordination on both Fort Sumner and White Oaks began in earnest.[81]

Garrett and Lea organized a posse. Through Wild's instructions, they drew a contingent from the Texas Panhandle to minimize possible leaks. However, there were some local residents entrusted with the work. Barney Mason, a resident of the Fort Sumner area, was known to both Garrett and Wild. They hired Mason as an informant to get close to the Dedricks at White Oaks, where he was not known. His cover was almost blown soon after his arrival, when he ran into the Kid, David Rudabaugh, and Billy Wilson at the livery stable. Recognized, Mason made up a story that he planned to steal some horses. The Kid was suspicious, but supposedly Sam Dedrick vetoed any inclination to shoot Mason at the time.[82]

Panic set in from both sides. Mason went straight to the local authorities and disclosed the Kid's presence in White Oaks, then vacated the community for safety in Roswell. While the authorities pursued the fugitives, Charlie Bowdre made a decision to leave Yerby's Ranch for Fort Sumner. He later wrote Joseph Lea that he did this as "a duty" to Thomas Yerby to prevent any possibility of an embarrassing raid there.[83]

Bowdre's purpose in writing Lea was to extricate himself from the Kid's current activities. He knew that Pat Garrett won the recent election as Lincoln County's sheriff, and replacing George Kimbrell in January. Lea was the newly-minted lawman's friend. A sympathetic figure by late 1880, Bowdre had split loyalties, but clearly wanted out of the criminal ring. This was confirmed by the scarcity of his mention in Wild's early reports, and by one of Garrett's own deputies.[84]

John P. Meadows was both a deputy and longtime associate of Sheriff-Elect Pat Garrett. In his collected reminiscences, Meadows detailed Garrett's encouragement to the Kid and others to leave the region. He highlighted his meeting with Bowdre in an undated parley on San Juan Mesa, east of the Pecos River. Although the manuscript indicated this meeting took place in spring or summer 1880, it was probably later. Based on the estimated dates of service in any law enforcement capacity, Garrett probably met Bowdre in early November, shortly after his meeting with Wild.[85]

> *Garrett arranged a meeting with Charlie Bowdre out on the San Juan Mesa. The agreement was that they were to meet unarmed and talk things over. But Bowdre came with his six-shooter on. Garrett did not like that, and he scolded Bowdre, saying "Look here, you've betrayed my confidence. You've come armed."*
>
> *But Garrett went ahead anyhow with the meeting. He said to Bowdre, "The best thing all of you boys can do is leave the country. Why don't you do like Frank and George Coe? Go off to one side and stay awhile; then come back when this thing is over."[86]*

According to Meadows, Bowdre agreed to Garrett's terms. The law was not on his side, and his level of criminal activity was far beyond his means to control, the cattleman planned an exit strategy.[87]

In early December 1880, violent activity followed the Kid and the counterfeit and rustling ring. Billy Wilson was in the wind, but mistakenly cast as a leader. As both were relative newcomers to the region, bad information was hard to Wild, nor easily denied by Wilson. By December 4, Wild spoke to Lea about the counterfeit operation, and learned he met with W.H. West. The businessman blamed Wilson for spreading the fake bills, and "revealed" to Lea he received one himself. In fact, both the Kid and Wilson served as little more than henchmen. The real leader of the counterfeiting operation was none other than the aforementioned West.[88]

On December 15, 1880, as both Wilson and the Kid dodged the law, Charlie Bowdre penned a desperate letter to Joseph Lea. According to publisher Phil Cooke in a letter to historian Robert Mullin, the *"Bowdre letter is the last of many he wrote Lea as Lea* stated in his. I still feel that the two of them add up that Bowdre was on the verge of selling out Kid. "[89]

Fort Sumner Dec 15 1880

Capt Lea

I have broke up housekeeping and am camping around, first one place and then another on the range, so that no one can say that Yerbys ranch is the stoping [sic] place for any one. So no party will any excuse for going there unless they are after me. I thought this a duty due Mr. Yerby, for if there is nothing to eat at the ranch no one will go there & there will be no chance for a fight coming off there & Mr. Yerbys property injured. If I dont [sic] get clear I intend to leave some time this winter, for I dont [sic] intend to take any hand fighting the territory, for it is a different thing from what the Lincoln Co war was. The only difference in my case to some of the officers in Lincoln Co, is that I had the mis-fortune to be indicted before the fight was over, & did not come under the Gov's pardon. It seems to me that this would come to their minds once & awhile, when they are running around after me, but I suppose it is human nature to give a man a kick when you have the upper hand. I saw the two Billies the other day & they say they are going to leave this country. That was my advice to them for I believe it is the best thing they can do. Don't you think if you can get the Gov' interested in my case, that it could be thrown out by the Dist' Att' without my appearing at court. I don't doubt your good intentions, but during the present state of the country

I think there is some danger of mobing [sic]. For my name has been used in connection with a good many things that I have nothing to do with, which outside parties can't know. I have taken your advice in regard to writing Mr. Yerby & have no doubt but what he *will do all he can for me. I know of nothing to urge in my favor, more than that others were pardoned for like offences, [sic] Experience is a good but short teacher & I think if I keep my mind, I will let every man do his own fighting so far as I am concerned & I will do my own.*

Respt

Chas Bowdre[90]

Bowdre's heartfelt letter arrived too late to do any good. Garrett's men appeared at Sunnyside. By this time, Bowdre joined the other fugitives and hid out in a small stone bunkhouse in nearby Stinking Springs. According to Charles Rudolph, Garrett's posse found no fugitives when they reached a snowy and cold Fort Sumner on December 19. After searching Beaver Smith's corral, Garrett learned the group left the area the day before. The angry sheriff-elect found Smith's employee Jose Valdez, a known friend of the Kid and his companions. He forced him to write a letter. The message told his adversary that Garrett and his men left the area, and that dinner awaited them. Although he initially resisted Garrett, Valdez acquiesced under pressure. He felt terrible afterwards.[91]

Once the trap was set, Garrett's men waited. As darkness fell, several riders approached the porch of the house. The lead rider was identified as Thomas O'Folliard. Once close enough, Garrett emerged on the porch and called on the young man to surrender. By instinct, O'Folliard reached for his gun. Garrett was ready for him and fired first, hitting his mark. However, the fugitive's horse bolted and carried him from the scene. The lawmen followed O'Folliard's painful moans, and he surrendered when found. The posse carried him back to the house and placed him on the floor. Tom O'Folliard died minutes later.[92] Others escaped in the darkness. One of them was "Dirty Dave" Rudabaugh, as Rudolph wrote of his wounded horse. The outlaw rode out to the Brazil-Wilcox ranch, where he abandoned the dying animal. Garrett's men followed, and learned the entire gang of outlaws passed through there. They correctly figured out the fugitives hid in the abandoned stone house owned by Alejandro Perea.[93]

Of the three outlaws interred in the cemetery at old Fort Sumner, O'Folliard was first and least celebrated. The lack of sympathy was evident in Rudolph's words. He wrote that O'Folliard was "unceremoniously" buried the day after his death, *with all his pursuers and a few villagers in attendance. He needed no eulogy; with all of his bravado and valor, he had gone the way of all murderers and thieves.*"[94]

Charlie Bowdre barely outlived his former employee. By nightfall, Garrett's men took positions at Perea's rock house at Stinking Springs. The snow and cold biting wind took their toll, but they spied the gang's horses outside. They waited until daybreak. Then, a lone figure emerged from the house with a bucket of corn feed for the horses. The posse opened fire, and the man dropped his bucket and grabbed his chest. He turned and limped back into the stone house. Rudolph wrote that the Kid shouted to Garrett from inside that Bowdre *"got a chunk of lead in him the size of a hen's egg and wants to turn himself in"* if they refrained from shooting.[95]

Garrett assented to the terms if no guns were present. Still, the bloodied Mississippian stumbled out of the stone structure wielding a rifle, but with raised arms. Louis Bousman, one of the possemen, rose from his position and steadied the gravely-wounded Bowdre to a blanket. Bousman recalled, *"He was shot in three places and was bleeding. He did not live but a few minutes."*[96] In several accounts, Bowdre turned to Garrett and uttered, *"I wish, I wish"* just before he died. Bousman does not mention this specifically, but Rudolph's memoir did. He may have uttered the words before his body was lowered to the blanket.[97]

Events unfolded starkly after Charlie Bowdre died. The Kid, Rudabaugh, Wilson, and Pickett held out until nearly dark. With no food and dwindling ammunition, there was little choice but to surrender. The posse took them—and the body of Bowdre—back to the ranch house under guard. The following morning Garrett, with posse members Bousman and James East, brought the body to Fort Sumner, where Manuela Bowdre waited in the snow. Bousman stated, *"We whipped up the horses when we passed her and ran right up to the door, and I and Jim East grabbed the body and took it in and put it on the table."*[98] The posse expected to get a reprisal from Mrs. Bowdre, but she saved most of it for the sheriff-elect. *"She cussed Pat Garrett out   He told her to go over and pick out a suit of clothes to bury her husband in and he would pay for it. He also had the grave dug."*[99]

From this point, the recorded events were shrouded in memory and possibly exaggerated by time. Supposedly Bousman and East ran with the frozen body of Charlie Bowdre into the house and promptly dropped it on the floor, further enraging his widow. She began throwing objects at them. After they departed, she supposedly refused the body to be taken for burial. While most restated that Bowdre was buried next to O'Folliard, two differing versions stated he was interred privately "somewhere near Bonito Canyon" or taken by Coe back to Lincoln County. Both alternate burial theories were refuted by both Coe's daughter and historians.[100]

The remainder of the Kid's short life, a little longer than six months, was well-known and only recounted in summary. Garrett brought his prisoners to Las Vegas, and then they proceeded by train to Santa Fe. There the Kid awaited trial. While in prison, he was interviewed by George Fitzpatrick, He denied being the leader of the gang, adding their hideout, *"...that Portales business, I owned the ranch with Charlie Bowdre. I took it up and was holding it because I knew a stage line would run by there, and I wanted to keep it for a station."*[101] Eventually, the Kid was tried in Mesilla, found guilty, and sentenced to hang in Lincoln. Well-known to history, the Kid was taken to Lincoln. He escaped imprisonment at the courthouse on April 28, 1881, killing his guards in the process. For several months, the Kid evaded capture. However, Garrett used his extensive web of contacts and learned he was at Fort Sumner.[102]

Sheriff Garrett, who wasted little time since his term began in January, cornered the Kid at Pete Maxwell's residence. He took a few select deputies, slipped into Fort Sumner and into the Maxwell residence. On the night of July 14, the Kid observed something amiss as he cut a slice of beef, and with a butcher knife in hand went to Pete's bedroom to ask about it-in Spanish. There the famed outlaw confronted Garrett for the final time, and he was shot in a darkened room as his pursuer crouched. Although one bullet struck a washstand, another found its mark.[103]

The sympathies of Pete Maxwell depended on who wrote the account. Bousman stated he wanted no part of hiding a fugitive. Rudolph never mentioned it. Maxwell administered Charlie Bowdre's estate, not his wife or a relative, as his former employer. Whether or not this was decided by Garrett or another official is not known.[104]

In Mississippi, Bowdre's family received word of Charlie's death a month later. The youthful Jose Valdez handled the task of explanation. There must have been instruction in such a case, as he knew to who and where to write. Donald McKay Dockery, Bowdre's brother-in-law, was the recipient of the news. The family felt it important of enough to type and copy the entire text of the message, and it has never been published.[105]

Fort Sumner, N.M.
Jan 16/80 [81]

Mr. D.M. Dockery
Hernando, Miss.

Dear Sir:

Your letter of inquiry in regard to the death of Mr. Chas. Bowdre rec'd. In reply would say that he was killed 14 miles East of this place about the 20th ult by a posse commanded by the sheriff of Lincoln Co., and a U.S. deputy marshall [sic] who carried wants [warrants] for him from Lincoln Co.

Bowdre at the time was with a party of men the most of whom were wanted by Territorial or U.S. officers among them Billy Bonny for whom a reward $500.00 was offered by Gov. Wallace.

They were surrounded in a small house in the night and in the morning Bowdre stepped outside and a volley was fired at him one shot of which took effect in the chest and one on the back of the head making a slight wound.

He ran into the house and by permission came out to talk to the sherriff [sic]. He however only articulated the words "I wish" and fell down and expired immediately. It is due Bowdre and the firing party to say that the latter mistook Bowdre for Billy Bonny [sic] their appearance [sic] being very similar and the early morning being Foggy. Had they known who it was the [they] undoubtedly would not have fired.

The balance of the party 4 in number stood out until near night and surrendered. Bowdre was at the time in charge of the cattle of Mr. T.G. Yerby and was living on his ranch. Bowdre was a man about 5 ft 7 or 8 inches in height, light complexion, blue or gray eyes and would [weighed] about 135 lbs.

Wore a mustache and goatee light in color – was well educated and a good writer and in general appearance [sic] was good looking. Hoping the above account will be satisfactory

I remain Respectfully,

J.L. Valdez
Fort Sumner, N.M.
San Megul [sic] Co.[106]

A careful analysis of this letter revealed some key findings. The young Valdez wrote legibly, but was not given to some of the technical terms within the document. The sentence structure was inconsistent, and the end of the letter took a different tone than the first five paragraphs. The latter part of the letter contained one-line, hastily-written descriptions, while the first paragraphs explained in ample detail. Lastly, there were some key misspellings and mistakes. The year of the letter was actually 1881, although it was January and this might have been an honest error. The misspellings were more common in the final portion of the letter. Therefore, the letter from Valdez to Donald Dockery was a partially-dictated note from Garrett or Lea. As Garrett had done this with Valdez before, when luring the Kid's party to Fort Sumner, he probably instructed the young man in the first paragraphs. The final portion might have been his own or a sympathetic friend, such as cowhand Bob

Campbell. The latter was an ally who passed information to the Kid.[107]

CHAPTER THREE

MATTERS OF THE GRAVE

The documentation on the death and burial of the Kid was at best an inconsistent affair. When asked by a researcher, historian Donald Lavash determined *"there seems to be no law governing a sheriff to file a certificate stating that he killed an outlaw"* after consulting the General and Compiled Laws of New Mexico.[108] Still, given the Kid's stature in the public eye, Garrett observed the necessity of a formal declaration. A hastily arranged coroner's jury, composed of several Spanish residents, drafted a judgement in their native tongue. For some time, this document went missing, stoking the idea that the dead body was not Billy the Kid, but a servant boy on the Maxwell Ranch. This was confirmed by a number of 1930s accounts undertaken by the Works Progress Administration, and by an admission by historian Maurice Fulton. He wrote to Robert Mullin in July 1953.

Weight of evidence is important in trying to sift fact from fantasy. During my first years of seeking information from old-time families in New Mexico the one statement I most frequently encountered, one on which there was unanamous [sic] agreement, notably among native families, was that the man shot in the dark of Pete Maxwell's bedroom was not William Bonney, later known as Billy the Kid.[109]

The coroner's report surfaced in the 1930s, according to a letter from Louis F. Rudolph Jr. to Historian Lavash. Rudolph, who at times spelled his name "Rudulph," was researching his own family's involvement in the burial.

I first learned of the paper from the book, "Violence in Lincoln County", by William Kelleher [sic]. On page 343 of the book, he talks about the paper having disappeared for many years, and "in the early 30's", having been found while Harold Abbott of the office of Commissioner of Public Lands, was classifying old records in the basement of the Capitol Building. Kelleher goes on to say that he got a copy of the paper from George Abbott, brother to Harold. But he gives no idea as to what then became of the original.[110]

The real source of the copy of the coroner's jury report was not actually William Keleher, but Colonel Maurice Fulton. In a 1951 article in the *El Paso Times*, Fulton maintained a copy for preservation for many years before turning it over to the Roswell Museum. The document became a point of contention, after William Morrison suspected the document was not recorded. Further, Morrison alluded that this may have been Garrett's way of avoiding a formal inquest. Fulton parried this, noting Garrett, with the help of lawyer Charles W. Green, presented the report to the prosecuting attorney in New Mexico's First Judicial District. Garrett received a total of $2,300 in reward money, mostly from towns across the Territory. $500 was allotted by state legislature, which would have been scrutinized before any payment was made.[111] Further, Fulton wrote to historian and bookseller Jeff Dykes the following year that the original had been in the records for *"the Office of the Secretary of the Territory in Gov. Hinle's [Hinkle's] time, but has since been lost or mislaid."*[112]

Documentation aside, the Kid was paid his last respects. Colonel Jack Potter, who moved to the Fort Sumner area as a young cowhand in 1884, learned that Sheriff Garrett ordered local Spanish workers to remove the roof of an abandoned building. From this roof, the workers extracted wooden planks for a makeshift coffin. Walter Noble Burns credited a worker named Domingo Lubacher (the family name was actually "Swerbecker") for the coffin. By the afternoon of the 15th, Potter contended they transferred the Kid's body from the Maxwell home into a worker's wagon, and formed a procession to the cemetery. Potter noticed almost everyone in town followed, including Beaver Smith and Jose Valdez, who rarely closed the saloon. A Texas man spoke at the funeral, and paid compliments to the Kid between biblical passages. According to Potter, the preaching citizen concluded, *"Billy cannot come back to us, but we can go to him and we'll see him again up yonder, Amen."*[113] Felisita Sandoval, the daughter of Domingo Swerbecker, recalled a wake for the outlaw took place at the Jesus Silva house.[114]

The newspapers immediately blared stories on the death of the Kid. In New Mexico Territory, the ownership of the print business often fell under the influence of partisans. Headlines reported William Bonney's death accordingly. Once Garrett gave notice of the Kid's death, articles on the subject appeared beginning July 18, 1881. The *Las Vegas Daily Gazette* was the nearest major town, and a telegraph there sent word through the Associated Press to newspapers across the country.[115] The *Las Vegas Optic*, a competitor newspaper in town, was responsible for much of the legend that came thereafter. The article headline from the issue of Monday, July 18, 1881, screamed: *"THE KID" KILLED! He meets His Death at the Hands of Sheriff Pat Garrett, of Lincoln County."*[116] An anonymous writer named "Ranchero" gave a description that echoed through subsequent texts.

...Pat went into Mr. Pete Maxwell's room to get what news he could of the "Kid," and he had not been there two minutes before the "Kid," in his stocking feet, entered the room and walking up to the bed on the edge of which Pat was sitting talking to Maxwell, with a pistol (self-cocker) in one hand and a big butcher-knife in the other.

Pat reached behind him for his pistol and at the action, "Kid" dropped his pistol on him and asked in Spanish "Quien es? Quien as?" This delay in firing on the "Kid's" part gave Pat all the time he needed, and the words were barely uttered before Pat's dauntless courage had driven a ball through the centre of the "Kid's" heart. He died in a moment, almost without a groan.[117]

The news report, particularly the *Optic* piece, was echoed in Pat Garrett's book. Given his background as a newspaper editor, Ashmun "Ash" Upson, a Roswell resident and jack-of-all-trades, served as Garrett's ghostwriter on most of the coming book-sized account. Was Upson also "Ranchero"? It was not an outrageous possibility. Even the "Ranchero" version prompted some questions and there appeared to be a hero-worship quality to it. Still, no other alternative spread as fast across national headlines. In subsequent decades, doubt and suspicion of the account of the Kid's death crept into print. His own subordinate, John Poe, posted outside the building during the incident, later fell out with Garrett. He challenged the account in his own memoirs. It was not just Poe who felt Garrett's official view was not accurate. Most of the Spanish families who knew the Kid spoke of the incident, and some saying Garrett killed the wrong person.[118]

The same shadow of suspicion marked the Kid's final resting place. Coupled with the lack of formal documentation and the impromptu funeral, it was further exacerbated by the presence of a rudimentary wood marker. In reality, wooden headboards were quite common for the time and place. The marker was ordered by Pete Maxwell the day after the service, and his workers pulled pieces from the fort's parade ground fence, and sawed off a part of one of them to fashion a cross. On the obverse of the marker was written, "BILLY THE KID, JULY 14, 1881."[119] In the upper left corner was an inscription done in hand: "Dormir bien querido" or "sleep well, dear one."[120] The rough-hewn marker enhanced the uncertainty of burial among some New Mexicans. Although several of the local residents, notably Paco Anaya, reinforced the claim that he and his fellow workers buried the famous outlaw.[121]

It was these local residents who burnished the legend of Billy the Kid. Anaya, a young sheep rancher at the time of the Kid's death, was a family friend who stayed with them at several key moments during his last few months of life, according to his son Louis. He came to Anaya's sheep camp and *"during the last 20 days he told him the complete Story [sic] of his life. It was during these discussions that Jesus [Paco Anaya's father] & Paco Anaya talked him into leaving the country But [sic] he had to see Pablita [Paulita] Maxwell one more time before he left."*[122] The Kid died shortly afterward. In 1930, once he realized the importance of his memories, Paco wrote his memories down in a 60-page manuscript in Spanish. He left the papers unpublished at his death in 1947, and the translated version was completed by publisher James H. Earle for his "Early West" series in 1991.[123]

Even after Paco Anaya and his companions completed his burial rites, news swirled around the Kid's grave site at the time. A January 1882 visit reported in the *Las Vegas Optic* foreshadowed the court battles to come. Entitled "The Bivouac of the Dead," it gives a lonely, grim description.

To the Southwest of the abandoned and decaying Fort Sumner lies the graveyard surrounded by what was an adobe wall, but from decay and neglect it is now only an outline around an acre of ground. We enter on the north, walking through the remains of a once handsome gate...

O'Folliard and Bowdre, who were killed by Pat Garrett and posse. These graves are all unmarked and that of Bowdre shows the scratching of some hungry coyote who seems to have been scared away by something before he reached his prey.

To the right of the entrance lies the grave of Billy the Kid marked by a plain board with the stenciled letters BILLY THE KID... [124]

Both time and theft assured an unmarked grave. Pete Maxwell lived in the old fort buildings for a time, but ownership changed. Manuel Brazil oversaw the family's horses, but indebtedness drove him out within a decade. Cowhand Jack Potter, who arrived in the area in 1884, observed that several pieces of Maxwell's cross, which looked more like the letter "T" to some, rotted near the bottom. Passing soldiers once used it for target practice and left about eight bullet holes. At the time Potter worked in Fort Sumner, where his employer, the New England Live Stock Company, acquired the land containing the complex and cemetery for its large spread. It was only then that one of its owners literally removed the marker, and shipped it east for "preservation."[125]

It was no accident there was so much interest in Fort Sumner land. The Maxwell Grant, named for Pete's father Lucien, was coveted for its water sources. Since the Maxwell family never obtained legal title to the reservation, it was eventually auctioned. A short distance away, the Chisum family wrestled with financial issues. "Cattle King" John Chisum died of cancer in December 1884, and his brother James and son-in-law William Robert risked strategies that left the field wide open for competition. Several independent Colorado-based ranchers bought large parcels of land, notably Sam Doss, Daniel L. Taylor and Lonny Horn.[126]

Of these named newcomers, Lonny Horn was the most familiar with the area. He was born in Lamar County, Texas in 1845. From an early age, Horn worked with his maternal Uncle Sam Doss in early cattle drives, and later moved to Trinidad, Colorado. It was said to be a forced move after Doss fatally shot a man in the Texas hill country by early 1871. During their journey, they came across Fort Sumner and saw potential. They formed a number of partnerships in the latter part of the decade, and Horn acquired a large herd and extensive land holdings in the region. His branded cattle herd numbered about 9,000 head by early 1882. His social position also improved after he became president of the Bank of Southern Colorado the following year.[127]

A partnership evolved to purchase the Fort Sumner Military Reservation containing the cemetery at auction. The holdings of Horn, Doss, and Taylor were complimented by those of John Lord, who represented the New England Live Stock Company of Greeley, Colorado. Connecticut native Alfred T. Bacon and his partner Luther D. Coggins incorporated the business in late 1881. Bacon's influential family lived in the same town as the family of Pat Garrett's friend Ash Upson, and had ample ties to Yale University.[128]

The New England Live Stock Company bought the Fort Sumner Military Reservation and the Maxwell holdings from the federal government on January 15, 1884. Over the next year, Bacon and his partners consolidated their holdings. As the new owners concentrated on the area, they homesteaded or brought in key personnel. Horn built "Pigpen Ranch" near Melrose, New Mexico Territory, with timbers from the Maxwell buildings. Jack Potter, who chronicled much of the activity during this period, was brought to Fort Sumner by Bacon a few months after the purchase as manager. In this capacity, he reported approximately 30,000 head of cattle in the company's Fort Sumner holdings. This included the partnering herds of Doss, Taylor, and Horn, who maintained their own brands. However, with the holdings of the New England Live Stock Company, Bacon and his brother-in-law Theodore S. Woolsey took on great debt, and needed more investors. In the late summer of 1885, a famous incident took place during a visit with potential investors, as later recounted by Jack Potter in a 1929 letter to Yale University President William Lyon Phelps.[129]

> *You wouldent [sic] think that Yale could be mixed up in the storie [sic] of Billy the Kid, how ever [sic] It Is [sic] a fact that Theodore Woolsey Jr, Alfred T Bacon and a Mr Chancey swiped The Marker [sic] from the Kids Grave [sic] this has puzzled Mabny [sic] a writer and I am the only living man that about It [sic]...these people came down to fort Sumner about the year 1885 to Inspect [sic] their holding after checking up on their holding[s] and ready to return to the Railroad [sic] which was three days drive they ask me to show them the Kids grave after lookingat [sic]*
>
> *It [sic] he says this is our land and our Cemetery [sic] and as the fence Is [sic] In [sic] bad repair and cattle rubing [sic] on those markers. I believe I will take this marker of the Kids a long [sic] and put it In [sic] a museum In [sic] Boston...[130]*

Potter could do little at the time. However, letters written between Bacon and Woolsey in 1885 detailed their visit to New Mexico Territory that summer, and he proved the accuracy of their former manager's memory. His subsequent quest for the marker 40 years later occurred after Charley Foor, one of the three men who buried the outlaw, took author Walter Noble Burns out to the cemetery. One of his contemporaries, John Roark, wrote Potter about the last public glimpse of Billy the Kid's burial marker in a 1930 letter.[131]

Am surprised at you trying to roundupas [sic] worthless piece of property as the Kids Marker. According to my memory It [sic] was the old Grizly [sic] hombre that hung onto the marker like a leach, Who [sic] claimed his camp was In [sic] the town of Boston, he taken great Interest In It [sic] and repaired It At The [sic] San Juan Dios Road house, first day out from Fort Sumner…I can well remember that It [sic] was strapped To [sic] Old Grizlie's baggage, I believe they called him Chancy or Chauncey.[132]

For Potter, despite his best efforts, the trail went cold. Billy the Kid's grave marker vanished with "Chauncey" back east in the summer of 1885.[133]

Fortunes declined for the New England Live Stock Company and others after the removal of the Kid's grave marker. The dreaded "Texas Fever" spread among the cattle herds, and Bacon wrote of more livestock deaths from "loco," which they contracted through a toxin found in grazing grasses. The three other partners experienced similar misfortune.[134] The shifting change in ownership and misfortune upset the social order of the area, and ultimately meant the departure of a number of ranchers and their families. Tom Yerby, Charlie Bowdre's former employer, intended to sell out to a Kansan named Russell. However, he held out until February 1888, when he sold out to the New England Live Stock Company. As historian Don Lavash discovered, prior to his departure in March for other regions, his Las Vegas residence became the property of his companion Nasaria Leyba. Ever the businessman, he noted the transfer was for "all services rendered," hinting they never married. In early 1892, financial hardship drove Manuel Brazil from the ranch where the Kid's gang spent a few desperate minutes before moving on to Stinking Springs. In a letter to Pete Maxwell's brother-in-law, Manuel Abreu, Brazil related his indebtedness to the Scottish Mortgage & Land Investment Company and intention to mine in Colorado.[135]

After additional financial reverses, the New England Live Stock Company and their partners lost their grip on their Fort Sumner holdings. In July 1892, an ill Samuel Doss, feeling the personal strain, threw himself in front of a train in Trinidad. His nephew Lonny Horn moved between Pigpen Ranch and Colorado for another decade until his death in March 1903. The New England Live Stock Company sold portions of their enterprise after a draught in 1892. Although Bacon repaid the company's debt two years later, little dividend was left to reward investors. Within a few years, he sold the company and reverted back to selling real estate in Colorado. In June 1901, Bacon died suddenly in Denver at the age of 47.[136]

In removing the marker, the New England Live Stock Company caused a great deal of confusion for those searching for the Kid's grave. There were other contributing factors. Flashfloods occasionally devastated the cemetery. In 1904, a particularly vicious flood washed through the grounds. The following year, the military ordered the exhumation and removal of soldiers to a national cemetery in Santa Fe. They moved the remains by March 1906. These events, coupled with the loss of the Kid's marker, caused disagreement between two living pallbearers from his funeral. Jesus Silva and Paco Anaya disagreed on the actual location of the plot. To settle the matter, they agreed to officially mark the gravesite between the two points.[137]

As long as the Kid's contemporaries lived, someone could find his burial place. Frank Coe was among the last of them, although he was never fully convinced his friend died there. During the final years of the Kid's life, the Coe family moved to another section of New Mexico Territory and returned after the cessation of hostilities. His granddaughter Nellie Ruth Jones recalled a story from her mother. In the winter of 1913, Frank heard a rumor that the Kid lived in California. Frank and his daughter Helena traveled there to follow up on the story.[138]

Mother said that...that in his mind he knew that Billy the Kid was killed at Fort Sumner, but that in his heart he hoped it wasn't true. And that when he would hear about someone who claimed to be Billy the Kid...he would suddenly take a trip in that direction...She said that, she never would forget, that they went looking in search of a fella who claimed to be Billy the Kid. She said they parked up at the top of a hill, and Granddad made his way down the hill, there was a little stream there, crossed it, and went over to this old cabin. He stayed quite a while, and when he came back, she said there were tears running down his cheeks, and he said it wasn't the Kid.[139]

The family of Charlie Bowdre had no reason to hope beyond the grave. Only a few years after Charlie's death, his brother Benjamin moved to Plumerville, Arkansas, approximately 40 miles west of Little Rock, with his brother Albert to open a mercantile business named Bowdre & Nesbitt. It was a successful enterprise, and later sold to a nephew, Bowdre Payne. One of the major streets of Plumerville was named for the family. Charlie's two brothers prospered. The ill fortune of their sibling was never discussed openly, but their knowledge of him was quietly passed through generations as a cautionary tale.[140]

Nashville Art Co. R. R. Photo Car.

Charlie Bowdre's younger brother Benjamin Bowdre kept in touch with his wayward sibling. He is pictured with his wife Noda Hull Bowdre and newborn son Paul, 1895.
Courtesy of Mrs. Betty Grabbe.

Before the late 1930s, the controversial burial arrangements at the old Fort Sumner cemetery resulted in little public tumult. Since local residents felt comfortable with the general location of the bodies, and someone could point it out. However, other changes, including natural causes and removal of some remains of the military dead, changed the landscape. A newer cemetery opened closer to the town of Fort Sumner, which grew out of the former Sunnyside. The old cemetery became a monument dedicated to the last chapter in the life of Billy the Kid. When those who knew, or believed they knew, where his body lay, passed on, controversy again set in. Their absence brought questions about the grave and who lay in it.[141]

CHAPTER FOUR

PUSH AND PULL

Beginning in the late 1920s, opinion on the legend of Billy the Kid divided between Lincoln County and the decade-old De Baca County, formed from parts of Guadalupe and Roosevelt Counties in 1917. The new jurisdiction was named for the second governor of the state of New Mexico, who passed away that year. The separation widened in the increasing glare of public interest. In 1926 and 1927, respectively, two major works appeared on bookstore shelves. The first was *The Saga of Billy the Kid* by renowned biographer Walter Noble Burns, and the other a new edition of Pat Garrett's *Authentic Life of Billy the Kid*, edited by Colonel Fulton. Both books ushered in a new era concerning the fate and burial of the famous outlaw. They followed generalized writings from the previous generation, such as Emerson Hough's *The Story of the Outlaw* and the fictionalized dime novels. The American reader thirsted for more factual information on Billy the Kid after reading the research gathered by Burns and Fulton, and this natural curiosity translated to television, movies, radio, and live entertainment. By the late 1940s and early 1950s, a slew of books sprang from this newfound popularity. It was only a matter of time before the discussion moved to the body in Fort Sumner. Eventually, that popularity prompted official fears and pitted one county against another for possession of the remains.[142]

The combined burst of media brought international attention to Billy the Kid. The Kid found new life as both hero and villain in cinemas and television. Dime novels and comic books appeared.

While the story of the Kid's death in Fort Sumner resounded overseas, the sleepy town itself gained little benefit from all the mass-media attention. While some increased tourism assisted, there was decades of economic decline. The focus of the Kid's legend remained in far-off Lincoln, primarily due to the distance and accessibility to the grave.[143]

However, the true threat to Fort Sumner was not a concern over economic decline in 1950. That paled in comparison to the claims of one Ollie "Brushy Bill" Roberts, who claimed to be Billy the Kid himself. To the residents of Fort Sumner, there was probably no greater insult to them. Roberts not only questioned their version of the legend, but the viability of whether the Kid's body lay in their cemetery. Although not intended as an additional slight, "Brushy Bill" was aided by one of Pete Maxwell's own relatives, William Vincent Morrison. As they gathered information, they visited the old cemetery, and he was pictured at the grave. "Brushy Bill" quipped they never really got him.[144]

"Brushy Bill" was a sensation when he emerged from the shadows in the summer of 1950. Morrison was a descendant of Ferdinand, the uncle of Pete Maxwell. Once convinced, he was a true believer. However, he was admittedly not a historian, but a legal professional in El Paso, Texas, far from Fort Sumner. Morrison had a knack for generating attention to his cause. When he advanced "Brushy Bill" Roberts for a pardon from Governor Thomas J. Mabry, he felt blindsided by the press and the son of the Kid's nemesis, Oscar Poe Garrett. The experience went badly when Roberts' memory blanked at times under intense and critical barbs. Failing to gain a pardon, the broken old man retired quickly, and died within weeks. The angry Morrison, consumed by guilt for the unexpected betrayal by Mabry, never forgave those responsible. He co-authored a book with Professor C.L. Sonnichsen, *Alias Billy the Kid*, in 1955. In the early 1960s, the old injury still stung.[145]

The general condition of the cemetery deteriorated as quickly as the appearance of "Brushy Bill." Long after Pete Maxwell lost the land and died in June 1898, the leadership of the Maxwell family fell to his sisters Odila Abreu and Paulita Jaramillo. Billy the Kid romanced Paulita at the time of his reported death.[146] In August 1938, Paulita's daughter Adelina Welborn pleaded for relief after the land containing the cemetery was sold by the county's irrigation district. She decried the sale in a printed handbill: *"Now can we allow greed to disturb all of our early traditions, and the respect of the coming generations, that should be accorded to the dead. Forty acres was set aside, for a cemetery, when Mrs. Maxwell sold the lands at the old fort."*[147] She recognized the twin dangers of apathy towards an active burial ground containing members of her family and a historically valuable landmark. The grounds were not active as a cemetery, although residents sought unoccupied plots for new interments. Burials fully ceased in 1946.[148]

Another reason for the deterioration of the Old Fort Sumner Cemetery was its weather-related events. Periodic flashfloods rendered a number of grave plots unrecognizable. In the 1920s, period photographs depicted visitors to the old cemetery in a field devoid of most landmarks. However, a local citizen with knowledge of the grave location was usually on hand. In the spring of 1930, Fort Sumner acknowledged an uptick in its tourism with an attempt to mark the grave. There was disagreement between the surviving members of the burial party over the precise location of the plots within the grounds, but they agreed over an approximate area. Jesus Silva and A.P. Anaya, both 72 years old, approached local handyman J. Thomas Perkins with a unique job. He placed concrete curbing in the area where the three plots of Billy the Kid, Charlie

Bowdre, and Tom O'Folliard were believed to be buried. The problem was that the two aging witnesses remained unsure of the exact location. However inexact the measurement, a monument was erected and dedicated to the three of them.[149]

The monument for the three Regulators was designated with their death dates and a single word "PALS" engraved above their names. J. Vernon Smithson described the monument in his April 1936 submission for the Works Progress Administration.

In a little unkept cemetery, dotted with crosses of many unknown graves, Billy the Kid lies in company with his two pals, Tom O'folliard [sic], and Charley [sic] Bowdre, who were killed a short time before Billy the Kid met his death...Enterprising citizens of Fort Sumner have erected a monument marking the graves...The three were buried side by side.[150]

Although the newest marvel, the monument was only one of the local attractions in Fort Sumner. In the 1920s, the Maxwell relatives celebrated the Kid's legend by bringing their artifacts into a museum. For a quarter's admission, visitors gazed on the historic treasures housed in the small building on Pete Maxwell's former property. His bed, washstand, and carpenter's bench were all present, as was the family piano purchased by their father Lucien after his return from the California Gold Rush. The washstand and carpenter's bench were of particular historical importance. Fatally wounded, the Kid lay dying on the bench, marked by faded bloodstains. A bullet hole penetrated the washstand, thanks to an errant shot of Pat Garrett. A Spencer rifle, allegedly gifted from the Kid, and a number of miscellaneous firearms and family photographs completed the exhibit. In time, the family museum folded, but it represented Fort Sumner's earliest recognition of a tourist attraction other than the cemetery. It was also the last gasp of influence the Maxwells exerted on the behalf of the property.[151]

Ironically, the fading fortunes of tourism in De Baca County, as exampled by the Maxwell family's museum, found an opposite experience in their counterparts of Lincoln County. Their families saw thriving tourism. The Coe Family, tied to the Kid through their friendship, passed on considerable influence to the next generation of their kin. Both Wilbur Coe and his wife Louise steered tourism to Lincoln County through political acumen and affinity for the arts. The couple saw the village's conversion from a remote ghost town to a restored center for art and history. Another advantage was their family's children. There were varying levels of interest in the Billy the Kid legend among them, but one of the children appeared to be the most determined to carry out her father's wishes. It was Frank Coe's daughter Helena Coe LaMay.[152]

In truth, the Coe homestead at Glencoe, located between San Patricio and the budding resort of Ruidoso, was an odd place to rebury the outlaw. However, the Coe cousins were among the Kid's staunchest allies in the Lincoln County War. George and Frank wanted his legacy preserved. They were less sure where to rebury him. Frank's aforementioned 1913 journey to California failed to end his curiosity. His son Wilbur recalled a 1925 trip in which his father inquired about the return of the Kid's body to Lincoln. *"Due to expense of the operation and poor transportation facilities he was unable to carry out"* the scheme at the time. The goal was the return of the body to the town of Lincoln, within proximity of his friends.[153]

In time, the Coes abandoned their plans to remove the Kid's body from Fort Sumner. Frank died in September 1931. George carried on for another decade. He widely imparted his views of Billy the Kid during his remaining years, and penned a well-known book,

Frontier Fighter. It saw publication in 1934. In the process of working with Nan Hillary Harrison on the seminal work, George spoke at the Alamogordo Chamber of Commerce with Almer N. Blazer, where the two recalled the mill battle where Charlie Bowdre first drew blood with the Regulators. By the time *Frontier Fighter* appeared in print, he numbered among the last survivors of the Lincoln County War. With George Coe's death in November 1941, the next generation carried on. They emerged as leading advocates of Lincoln County history—and the legend of Billy the Kid.[154]

The excitement over the appearance of "Brushy Bill" Roberts similarly affected the Coes, Lincoln County, and the rest of New Mexico. While gathering support for Roberts, William Morrison reached out to Helena LaMay in April 1950. He noted tensions the subject brought to New Mexico. She responded: *"As for creating dissention: that is the easiest thing to do here on the river. Just mention Billy-the-kid and interest perks up immediately. Even in high school sides are still well marked."*[155]

The Coe family represented part of the initial vanguard in the restoration and festival plans formulated by the Old Lincoln County Memorial Commission and the Lincoln County Historical Society. The aging structures in the town of Lincoln, some in miserable shape, were irreplaceable landmarks. Their preservation was necessary. The courthouse, formerly the Murphy-Dolan store, was the historical center of activity during the days of Billy the Kid. The Torreon, the circular fortress structure built to repel Indians and store vital supplies, was another local landmark during the Lincoln County War. Both places needed restorative work. Concerned historians, led by Colonel Fulton, banded together with regional and community leaders in the creation of a nine-person commission focused on preservation. Fulton saw the heavy economic price paid by Fort Sumner in the preceding decades, and he feared the same fate for Lincoln.[156]

The Old Lincoln County Memorial Commission was a unique organization when formed in 1949. Internal dissention led to roster changes over a short period of time. This created an atmosphere that at times lacked decisive direction. Fulton was the primary historian and executive secretary in its early days. He was augmented by the region's "movers and shakers." Some were not residents of Lincoln County, including Eddy County's Harold D. Miller as chairman and Chaves County's Jim Cooley as secretary-treasurer. Lincoln was represented by Vice-Chairman Albert "Bert" Pfingsten. In doing so, the restoration of Lincoln became a state concern. The well-to-do people of the region involved themselves in the spirit of the project, which added long range goals for records preservation and assistance to local historical societies. Each member was appointed by the governor and considered a state steward.[157]

Changes in personnel occurred by the late spring of 1950. Colonel Fulton provided vital energy to the new organization, but acknowledged the Commission raised hackles with the Lincoln County Historical Society.

Our Commission has been a straggly affair, hardly a quorum-size meeting without proxies. Hence no continuity of policy. The Commission has the hostility of the Lincoln County Historical Society, practically defunct, but able to kick up a fuss. Chat is what has happened, and I have been the target. When I came away, taking my own amassings with me largely, this organization spread the report that I was taking away valuable historical material belonging to the Old Courthouse. The Commission at a recent meeting on a very unrepresentative character raised the question whether I could be employed as researcher unless I lived at Lincoln, and also another point whether the budget could be adjusted to permit my modest salary to be paid. While these matters were being threshed out with Santa Fe, they suspend from office without salary...Fine treatment indeed![158]

Fulton worried over a planned presentation to the state legislature. The fledgling organization needed more defined powers if any support could be gleaned from them. However, other political issues distracted Santa Fe.[159]

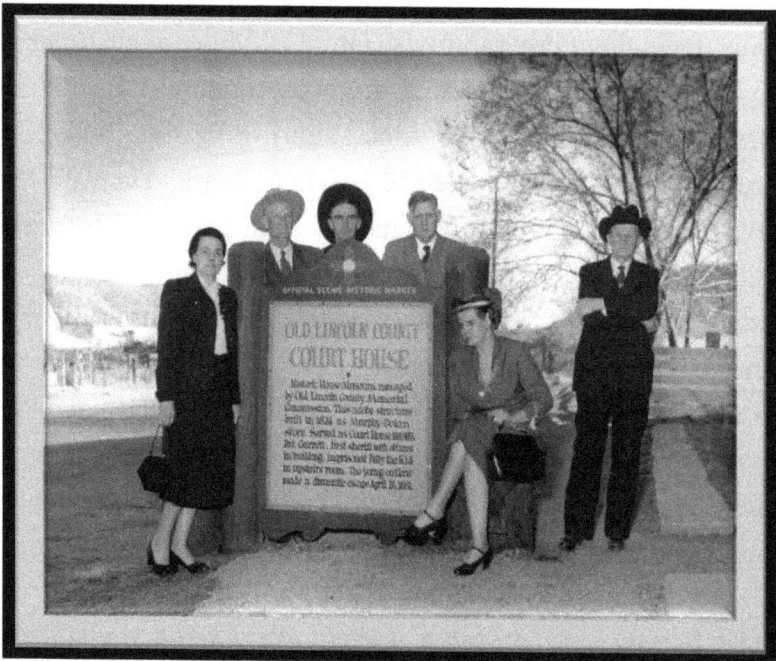

Members of the Old Lincoln County Commission, 1954. Historian William Keleher is third from right.
Lincoln County Collection, Courtesy Palace of the Governors Photo Archives (NMHM/DCA 104886).

In January 1951, Fulton was suddenly pushed out of the Old Lincoln County Memorial Commission. His contract mysteriously ended "on terms agreeable to both parties."[160] His fears of competing interests were proven to be founded. Only two months later, the New Mexico Legislature passed SB213, which prohibited changes in or to the Lincoln County Courthouse without the consent of the Commission. This was apparently due to a contentious battle about personally-owned historical items brought in by Fulton, including a copy of Walter Noble Burns' *Saga of Billy the Kid* with handwritten comments by Lily Casey Klasner. He obtained this while conducting research on a discarded book project. Although Fulton neglected to take the book home when he left the Commission, he had trouble getting the book back. In July, historian and lawyer William A. Keleher, who had been present during the "Brushy Bill" Roberts visit to Santa Fe, was appointed in his place.[161]

Colonel Fulton's departure ushered in major changes to the Old Lincoln County Memorial Commission. The custodial overhaul at the county courthouse brought the arrival of John and Nan Boylan, who directed the Lincoln Restorations Project. The powerful couple acquired and restored a number of the town's historic structures under state supervision. Aside from the courthouse, they reconstructed the Wortley Hotel, where Robert Olinger ate his last meal before his death at the Kid's hands. The re-development of the Hulbert and Watson Houses, and the exhibit in the Tunstall Store, were achievements of the Boylans. The composition of the Commission changed as well. In 1954, members posed for cameras in front of the new "official scenic historic marker" for the Old Lincoln County Court House. By then, the membership was more localized: Keleher, Pfingsten, Colonel Ewing Lusk of the New Mexico Military Institute, Mrs. Ora Lee Skipworth, Frank Mahill, and Mrs. Dessie Sawyer. This powerful group, particularly Keleher, Pfingsten, and Sawyer, would be the stable power centers of the organization for the next decade.[162]

While the Commission focused on preservation, Wilbur Coe and the Lincoln County Historical Society fostered a local pageant that became larger by the year. In 1940, the Coronado Cuarto Centennial Anniversary was observed throughout the State of New Mexico. The common theme focused on the first Spanish settlement, and approximately 200 folk festivals sprouted up in New Mexico communities. The feature presentation, "The Coming of Coronado," opened in Bernalillo, a town north of Albuquerque. Several large festivals extended into the summer. One of these was "A Day in Old Lincoln," which featured a Mexican wedding at the Isaac Ellis house, an arts and crafts demonstrations, and a dramatic play based on Philip Stevenson's "Sure Fire: Episodes in the Life of Billy the Kid." In the final event, the court house and jail became part of the stage on June 23rd.[163]

"The Last Escape of Billy the Kid," as the play came to be called, was the core of the "Pageant." The first version of the cast featured renowned San Patricio resident artist Peter Hurd as Billy the Kid. At 35 years of age, he was too old for the part despite his own youthful appearance. His colorful watercolors and pastels of local landmarks seemed to catch the crevice of each mountain. Even the charcoal drawings of local people resonated in the public's fascination with the history of the area. Next to the Kid, Hurd and his wife were arguably Lincoln County's most famous people at the time. In fact, he was once an apprentice to Henriette Wyeth Hurd's father, Pennsylvania artist Newell Convers Wyeth, before the 1929 marriage. Through the Pageant and his art, Hurd cemented his connection to Billy the Kid. The drama was so popular in its initial run that it repeated annually. However, Hurd's role as the Kid was replaced by other citizens.[164]

Peter Hurd connected his art with Lincoln County's preservation force in other ways. He was aided by the regenerated interest in general tourism of the Old West, local artists assembled in the Land of Enchantment in colonies. The Hurds settled at their San Patricio estate, which was complete with polo field, and brought both celebrities and like-minded artists to the region. Among the new artists to Lincoln County was John Liggett Meigs, an eccentric artist with an odd story. Born in May 1915, Meigs began life in Chicago, Illinois. His successful stockbroker father decided to leave his wife for another woman, and he took his infant son with him. The three of them travelled across the country under assumed names. His restrictive and temporary environment continued until he reached adulthood. After he finished high school in California, Meigs became a reporter in Hawaii. After the bombing of Pearl Harbor, he joined the Navy. He wrote home for his birth certificate, and only then learned his unique origins.[165]

After the war, Meigs returned to Hawaii and designed artistic leisure shirts. The clothing line was wildly successful, and his designs garnered large-scale attention. Peter Hurd came across the young Meigs on a visit to Hawaii in 1950. The two artists hit it off, and Hurd asked him to come work on a mural in New Mexico. The following summer, Meigs moved to San Patricio as Hurd's protégé. After his initial apprenticeship and a few years traveling and working abroad, Meigs returned permanently to live in San Patricio. In January 1953, he purchased an adobe structure near the edge of Hurd's ranch for $90. Over time, Meigs built multiple additions and grottoes to it. The ever-growing structure was known as "Fort Meigs."[166]

In Lincoln County, the mercurial Meigs was everywhere. His influence was known throughout the area in architecture, theatre and painting. He collected rare books, a lifelong obsession which eventually overwhelmed Fort Meigs. In May 1960, Wilbur Coe decided to hire Meigs as general manager and director of the

Pageant. He wrote Keleher of his plans to move the dates of the Pageant and the new hire.

Since talking to you in Albuquerque Monday night, realizing how difficult it may be to secure an all-round man to put on the Pageant this August 5, 6, 7, 1960, we think that as a General Manager and Director of the Pageant, Johnny Meigs, San Patricio, N.M., would be the best for the job...We are not sure that Johnny Meigs will be interested but if you think it advisable you might have John Boylan contact him.[167]

Meigs, through a Memorandum of Understanding between the Lincoln County Historical Society and the Old Lincoln County Memorial Commission, began his career as manager and director of the Pageant for a $300 salary, plus 10% of net proceeds. His involvement with the integrated twin efforts of restoration and tourism was never lost. Meigs later recalled the overall effort to re-create Lincoln into a "Williamsburg" of the Old West, like that town of the Revolutionary War era.[168]

As restoration and Pageant plans blossomed, conflict occurred between old and new residents and their respective concerns. John and Nan Boylan founded Lincoln's community library in 1960, located in the old Tunstall Store with some 3,000 circulating volumes and a full reference section for research. They planned extensive interviews with older residents. However, those goals clashed with those of other residents already in town. Roman Maes, the scion of a local Spanish family, was a frequent target of the Boylans. His wife Theodora was from the Romero family, whose parents owned the town store. Through the Romeros and his family, Roman Maes accumulated an impressive collection of old Lincoln artifacts. This included tintype images, "six-shooters," and other memorabilia from the period that Billy the Kid lived. In 1932, the artifact collection was added to the front of an existing saloon, known as the "La Paloma." The Maes owned it since 1923, keeping a well-stocked backroom bar for live music and dances. They lived next door to the business. The Maes occasionally added to the history exhibits, even a stagecoach from Kansas. Lincoln resident Joe Salazar recalled that one of the exhibit's guns belonged to Roman Maes' great-uncle. The Maes exhibit drew interest from the rich and famous. Actress Lucille Ball, musician Johnny Cash and actor Douglas Fairbanks, Sr. were all visitors to the La Paloma.[169]

The two different representations of museum clashed. The Old Lincoln County Memorial Commission initiated court action against Maes in August 1953, when both sought title of land adjoining the courthouse. The awkward relationship between the two enterprises wound through the courts for years.[170] In July 1960, the battle grew personal. On Commission letterhead, Mrs. Boylan wrote District Attorney Dan Sosa in Las Cruces, forwarding him a letter from "several persons of the Lincoln community" that objected to the loud music at the bar. In short, she sought their assistance in withholding permits for the dances.

Some time ago I talked to you on the telephone relative to the disturbance of a dance which had just been held at the bar. At that time you mentioned that you had instructed the justices of the peace and sheriff of Lincoln County not to issue any more permits for dances at the La Paloma Bar unless the proprietor, Roman Maes, brought suit in district court to force their issuance.

Nevertheless, the dances have gone on as before, apparently without Mr. Maes' having had a bit of trouble procuring the necessary permit.[171]

Joe Salazar remembered that some Lincoln residents were upset by parked cars on both sides of the town's main street near the courthouse. The crowd could get rowdy in any drinking establishment. There were claims of the drunken shouts from departing patrons disturbing the sleep of neighbors and broken bottles along the street. Both instances, particularly the concerns about their effect on future tourism, fueled Boylan's efforts. The newly-restored Wortley Hotel was within close proximity of the La Paloma. She was concerned the partying inhibited the viability of the historic establishment. Nan Boylan cited a stabbing during a dance held at the La Paloma in a letter to Keleher. She mentioned possible disruption of the forthcoming annual pageant. However, her fears were not realized and the La Paloma continued in its dual capacity for several years after this event.[172]

If the Lincoln land squabbles were not difficult enough, new trouble came from a completely different historical angle. The English Westerners' *Brand Book* from December 1957-January 1958 contained an article by meticulous researcher Philip J. Rasch entitled "Clues to the Puzzle of Billy the Kid." The article contained a paragraph which foretold his fascination with a possible descendant of the long-dead outlaw.

The writer has been in touch with a Miss Lois Telfair [sic], who states that she is a relative of the Kid. Correspondence with her brought out the fact that she is preparing an article on his early history which she will document with family records. All that she is willing to say at present is that he was born in Brooklyn in 1859, the son of William Bonney and Catherine McCarty.[173]

Aside from misspelling Lois Hanford Telfer's name, it was the first known published mention of her presence. Rasch lived on the east coast, so his initial acquaintance with her was not a surprise.

Ramon Mae's La Paloma Bar (and Museum) in Lincoln, ca. 1960
Courtesy of the Historical Society for Southeast New Mexico

Lois Telfer, 52, was a red-headed beautician living in New York City. From the beginning, she was not shy about her family connection to the Kid. She embraced her Michigan childhood and her Great-Grandfather Orris Bonney with free discussion. She admitted that much of her initial information came from her grandmother—and Orris' daughter--Celinda. She claimed her ancestor was a twin to the father of Billy the Kid. The twin boys, according to Telfer, were born in July 1826 in Lyons, Wayne County, New York. Her father moved to Michigan, and Celinda Bonney was born and raised there. She married Richard Warner of Grand Rapids, where that side of her family resided. In July 1905, their daughter Emma married Eugene Telfer, a coffee company executive based in Detroit. Although the Telfers were Canadian, they were prominent and wealthy when the Telfer Coffee Company emerged in 1899.[174]

Telfer's own family story started as decades of prosperity, but followed by sadness and separation. She was born on August 7, 1906 and named for her paternal grandmother. She attended Northern High School in Detroit, as did her brother Richard, two years her junior. Eugene Telfer became a civic leader as his management of the wholesale beverage business. She was mentioned in the local press. Sadly, her father's drinking problems ultimately led to marital problems. His half-brother eventually took over in his position, and Emma Telfer was a widow by the 1950s. Lois left Michigan permanently, and moved to New York to work as a beautician.[175]

Telfer adjusted to the fast-paced New York life, and she made influential friends. At the urging of her friend Sylvester Vigilante, the librarian of the American History Room at the New York Public Library, she researched her famous relative. Vigilante, who most called "Vig," was an author himself. His excellent work was exampled in several volumes of the "You Were There" history series of books for young adults. A native New Yorker from the city's lower east side, he grew up with 12 siblings and earned money shining shoes and lighting stoves. His tailor father moved the large family to Brooklyn. Vigilante worked in the branch library, but transferred to the New York Public Library as a page in 1909. From then until his retirement from the American History Room, he purchased books and photographs for the collections. Along the way, he developed a reputation for assisting historians and authors alike in historical research. His daughter Enid remembered that their home was filled with books, "*most with acknowledgements and personal notes from the authors.*"[176] In fact, Vigilante's house was an informal salon, with noted literary visitors on Sundays that dined on Italian dinners with wine. Although she does not specifically remember Lois Telfer, Enid recalled *"talking about a woman with fire-red hair, who was trying to exhume Billy the Kid. Don't know how that ever turned out."*[177]

Sylvester Vigilante encouraged Lois Telfer to visit New Mexico, but exhumation was not a discussion point in the late 1950s. When she finally made the trip in the late spring of 1959, her first sojourn included stops at Lincoln and Fort Sumner. In Albuquerque, she surprised William Keleher, who promptly wrote his friend Robert N. Mullin.

She [Telfer] had confusing bits of information, claiming most of them came from her Grandmother. She wanted to know how to get to Lincoln by bus, and I routed her via Socorro on one bus, change to the mail coach there, via Carrizozo and on to Lincoln.

She also wanted to get to Ft. Sumner, which she eventually reached via Roswell, and on Memorial Day, laid a wreath on his grave.[178]

As a result of this exchange, Mullin opened a correspondence with Telfer. In a rare admission, the historian admitted that his interest in Billy the Kid originated with Pat Garrett. He hoped that Telfer might reveal some long-sought answers to the Kid's origins, and he offered to visit her in New York. In August, the red-headed beautician wrote back. Not only had she planned a scrapbook, but rattled off a number of ancestral names and specific dates.[179]

In August 1959, few historians questioned Lois Telfer's claim. Phil Rasch, whose dogged curiosity often drew scorn from his contemporaries, was a rarity. He mailed her news reports and visited Lincoln shortly after her return to New York. Another historian, Leslie Traylor, showed Rasch letters with questions concerning her visit. Perhaps sensing an avenue of opportunity, he asked Telfer some of his own questions. In time, the brusque nature of Rasch's requests aliened him from his new correspondent.[180]

The May 13, 1960 issue of the *Albuquerque Journal* trumpeted Lois Telfer's story all over New Mexico. She was "discovered" the previous year, but known by then. Only two weeks stay in the "Land of Enchantment," and her name appeared in a reporter's column. Since she knew publicity was inevitable, Telfer embraced a mission to change minds about Billy the Kid. For example, one news story started with the byline "He Had Friends and Was Not Evil, Says Kid's Red-Haired 'Cousin.'"

Miss Lois Telfer, a cosmetologist for a French perfume manufacturer, said she visited at Fort Sumner and at Lincoln near Carrizozo with descendants of many residents of the area in the Kid's day who spoke well of the outlaw. She pointed out that Billy once tended Frank Coe, a Lincoln County rancher who was seriously ill, until he recovered.[181]

During her second visit, most residents welcomed her. In fact, it created lasting friendships. A request for family records in Carrizozo was forwarded to Helena Coe LaMay. Upon meeting the affable LaMay, the two ladies "hit it off." Her daughter Nellie Ruth Jones remembered Telfer as the "red-headed woman," and witnessed the long hours the two "*enjoyed talking about Billy the Kid.*"[182] LaMay not only hosted Telfer, but took her on a guided tour of Kid-related sites in the county. This included Fox Cave, nicknamed "Billy the Kid's Cave." Although legend had the cavern as the outlaw's alleged hiding place, Nellie Ruth Jones doubted "*he ever spent a night in it.*"[183]

Although warmly received throughout the trip, Lois Telfer unexpectedly found herself at the center of an advertising campaign in Lincoln. She posed for a newspaper photographer with local

Pageant actor John Thomas, who portrayed Billy the Kid. Both wore cowboy hats and sported six-shooters at the historical marker for the Wortley Hotel. The building was recently restored. The Telfer and Thomas image advertised the "Last Escape of Billy the Kid" and was published in several newspapers across the state. In addition, the accompanying article gave details about the newly-restored buildings and the Pageant.[184]

In truth, the press campaign did little. The Lincoln Pageant struggled financially by the end of 1960. John Meigs sounded the alarm that more monetary support from the state was vital to the decades-old tradition. He wrote that the *"only hope of survival of the famous event will be support by the State Legislature and the State Tourist Bureau which must decide its value as a tourist attraction..."*[185]

Although quiet for the first few months of 1961, a storm brewed over tourism dollars in both Lincoln and Fort Sumner. The undercurrent of financial insecurity, combined with local politics and personal suspicion, led to bad feeling between the two communities. Where they once shared pieces of the legacy of Billy the Kid, the weighty presence of Lois Telfer represented a tip of the scales. The aggressive restoration plans of influential citizens in Lincoln, through the Lincoln County Board of Commissioners, and the reactionary nature of De Baca's Board in kind, finally brought about an inevitable battle.

The origins of dissention between Lincoln and De Baca Counties over the corpse of Billy the Kid began on April 11, 1961. Three Lincoln County Commissioners: Chairman Kenneth Nosker, Charles A. Jones, and Ignacio Torrez, listened to the arguments of an influential group of citizens.

New Yorker Lois Telfer on a visit to New Mexico.
Courtesy of Nellie Ruth Jones.

The group's leader was Joe O. Sargent, a 40-year-old Texas transplant who represented the commerce office in Carrizozo, and their issue was the return of Billy the Kid's remains. His argument centered around two primary points. Firstly, the move assisted the county's upgraded preservation and Pageant experience plans, and secondly, De Baca County seemingly cared little about the current gravesite. Sargent easily made his first point to the Commissioners, as they were all equally invested in the Kid's legend. In fact, they knew about the historical advantages through their own families and communities. For example, Nosker was related to the Coes through his in-laws, while the Torrez family lived in the Hondo and San Patricio areas, where many descendants of Bonney's friends resided. However, the second point was a bad assumption. While little change occurred at the gravesite in Fort Sumner, the site was still sacred to many in De Baca County. Paul Baker, the publisher of the *Lincoln County News*, publicized the results of the conference and subsequent letter to the Board of Commissioners in De Baca County.[186]

The full text of the letter read as follows:

Gentlemen:

It has come to the attention of the Board of County Commissioners, Lincoln County, at several times in the past, that the grave of William H. Bonney, alias Billy the Kid, is being unduly exploited by Highway advertising signs in a manner that is offensive and not in good taste. Also, that the advertising and publicity refers to the Fort Sumner area as being the home of Billy the Kid.

The old Lincoln County Courthouse at Lincoln, New Mexico was Where William H. Bonney was sentenced to hang for the murder Of Sheriff Brady.

The Courthouse, which is administered by the Old Lincoln Memorial Commission, a State Agency, has many momentos of Billy the Kid and the Lincoln County War in which he took a leading part. Lincoln County was more a home of the Kid than anywhere else in the southwest.

There is enacted each year at Lincoln, New Mexico a pageant, "The Last Escape of Billy the Kid", and in its exciting sceans [sic] the good as well as the bad in the Kid is portrayed. It is entirely fitting therefore that the body of the southwest's Foremost personality not be subject to exploitation for Monetary purposes, rather that it be re-interred in its rightful resting place in Lincoln County, enshrined as his family and friends would have wished.

To this end we respective seek the cooperation of the Board of County Commissioners of De Baca County.

Respectively yours,

Kenneth Nosker, Chairman
Lincoln County Board of Commissioners[187]

The letter, dated April 11, 1961, was mailed to Fort Sumner by special delivery. County Clerk Judy Marshall registered its arrival in the De Baca County Commissioner's Journal. Chairman Robert J. Colter made no immediate public comment, except that the board considered the letter, and decided to think it over before submitting a response.[188]

In hindsight, the tone of the letter flared tempers in De Baca County. Although the Lincoln County Commissioners veered little from the truth about the condition of the gravesite, they viewed it differently. They felt they relieved the citizens of Fort Sumner a costly financial burden. If the body was moved, it defrayed any cost to restore the cemetery. However, they misjudged the community pride in the site. The letter's words hit pretty hard.[189]

The edited version of the letter in the *Lincoln County News*, combined with an editorial by Baker, was probably the last straw. Baker, who was considered a member of the group seeking the body of the Kid, pulled no punches in the editorial. Entitled "Let's Settle This Matter for All Time," he stated the general goals of the group, which were only partially reflected in Nosker's letter.

The Lincoln County Board of Commissioners is to be commended for the action taken last Friday in passing a resolution calling for the removal of the remains of Billy the Kid to their rightful resting place at Lincoln town in Lincoln County.

The County Commissioners adopted the resolution directed to the
Board of Commissioners of De Baca County, after a conference with
interested citizens, including Joe O. Sargent of Carrizozo.

Garish highway advertising signs directing the curious to the lonely
grave of Billy the Kid on the outskirts of Fort Sumner, have long been a
source of irritation to Lincoln County people; also, the claim of that area
as being "The Home of Billy the Kid."[190]

The first portion of Baker's editorial sent a message to the De
Baca County Commissioners. By disparaging their billboards, they
insulted those they hoped would cooperate with them. That was
probably not their intention, as Baker buried their primary motive at
the end of the editorial after a few paragraphs with historical
information.

The Old Lincoln County Courthouse Museum at Lincoln has a great
deal of material, both visible and written, concerning the life of this young
man who lived part of his life within the law and part of it outside. At
Lincoln, students of history, writers of fiction and history, as well as
interested tourists, can get first-hand information about Billy the Kid and
all participants in the Lincoln County War.

They can also view, in August, the thrilling pageant of events leading
up to the Three-day Battle, The [sic] Kid's arrest and his dramatic escape
from the hangman's noose.[191]

Baker's chief argument, similar to the adage "a rising tide lifts
all boats," came well after the stinging criticism. The actual goal of
the publicity was to show that Lincoln County had the resources and
will to care for the proposed gravesite. Had the presentation been
more nuanced or delicate, there may have been only muted
argument if De Baca County agreed. Although not all Baker's fault,
the bad diplomatic effort was clearly found in the official letter. The

last paragraph of the editorial endorsed the move of the body, but again castigated the highway billboards and signs.

> *What could be more fitting than that The [sic] Kid's remains be returned to Lincoln, to be reinterred in a plot of ground, in a landscaped "Billy the Kid Park?"*
>
> *His grave would have a dignified setting, entirely away from outlandish advertising on highway signs; or such a spectacle as at Boot Hill in Tombstone, where the graves of the just and the unjust are alike exposed to public ridicule.[192]*

The De Baca Commissioners reacted within weeks, and they signaled their outrage. They answered Lincoln's missive with their own. Their response contained intentional insults, which signaled they welcomed a fight.

Hon Board of County Commissioners
Lincoln County
Carrizozo, New Mexico

Gentlemen
> *Your letter of April 11th regarding Billy the Kid has been read and carefully considered.*
>
> *Our first thought was that your interest in your late citizen is somewhat delayed. After all, Billy the Kid was shot in 1881, now after 80 years you become concerned about him. Some deliberation is in order before a public body, such as the County Commissioners, can take an action, but to wait 80 years ----.*
>
> *Your letter also manifests concern about "exploitation" of Billy the Kid for monetary purposes. We certainly deplore any such mercenary approach to our history. If Lincoln County has been able and successful in preventing commercial exploitation of its history, we would be very glad to learn the methods used by you in preventing such sordid practices.*

History records that Billy the Kid was shot here – which saved Lincoln County the trouble and expense of trying and hanging him. Surely this favor on the part of De Baca County deserves some better repayment than your demand that his body be exhumed and sent back to Lincoln County. For shame, after offering the body of William H. Bonney refuge [here] for 80 years, we are not about to surrender it to his "Friends and Relatives" who have waited this long time to come forward and identify themselves.

In brief, gentlemen, your request is denied. And any other outlaws or criminals from your county who would seek refuge here can take warning from the fate of William H. Bonney, alias Billy the Kid.

Sincerely yours
Robert J. Colter, Chairman
Board of County Commissioners
De Baca County, New Mexico[193]

Both counties held their meetings on the same day--May 4, 1961. Commissioner Colter's response drew the expected reaction. However, his letter contained some historic inaccuracies. A formal request for a body does not equate historical reverence or concern. Additionally, De Baca County did not exist as a jurisdiction in 1881, so it was only since 1917 that Lincoln County inquired of that governmental body. The aforesaid 1925 removal plan by Frank Coe was well publicized, and that also indicated that concern began long before 1961. Although it never happened, there was no known rancor in De Baca County at the time. Commissioner Colter was more on point with his view on exploiting "commercialization," of which both jurisdictions were guilty. In different formats, both relied and needed the tourism dollars. Colter's reference to "outlaws" seemed more personal. The Lincoln group viewed Billy the Kid as more of a misunderstood cowhand than a villain. Only four days after the public letter, Commissioner Nosker and the two co-directors of the Carrizozo Chamber of Commerce, Sargent and Will Ed Harris, fired back a response.

The attitude you people have displayed concerning the re-interral of "Billy the Kid" is a little disappointing to us, inasmuch as you refer to him as a criminal and an outlaw. You seem to have some monetary reason for wanting him to remain in DeBaca County, certainly there is evidence of no other motive, judging by the type of highway advertising, as well as the condition of his grave.

You have mentioned the time element as a factor in your refusal to exhume the body. May we remind you that in certain cases that time is the only re-deeming [sic] feature. In spite of our great democratic system, history is cluttered with cases of injustice. And we in Lincoln County feel that Wm Bonney is a prime example. The Governor, Lew Wallace, offered amnesty to "the Kid" indicates that he had his good points. His refusal of amnesty which "laying down his arms" was a condition, is clearly understandable because of his fear "that he would never see the next sun." Perhaps you people in De Baca County can think of a better reason.

As to your request about successful methods used by Lincoln County, we would be most happy to have you examine one of the finest systems in New Mexico. You state that DeBaca County saved Lincoln County the trouble and expense of hanging and burying Billy the Kid. We, in Lincoln County, are grateful for anything that DeBaca ever did for us and we would be happy to refund any money that DeBaca was out in shooting and burying our "late citizen." Our records show that Ft. Sumner was a part of Lincoln County at that time. Could your records indicate otherwise?

May we also take this opportunity to place you on notice that the fate of "Billy the Kid" has not been entirely settled, especially in regard to his final resting place.

This movement has reached County-wide proportions and we have found it Necessary to create a special committee. The Chambers of Commerce in Carrizozo, Ruidoso and Capitan, as well as the Lincoln County Historical Society and the Lincoln County Commissioners, have appointed Joe O. Sargent to represent them.   And any Future correspondence you may have on the subject please direct it to him.

May we ask you again to reconsider our request or we shall be forced to take a more positive action.

Sincerely yours

Kenneth Nosker, Chairman
Lincoln County Commissioners

Joe O. Sargent, Director
Carrizozo Chamber of Commerce
Box 425, Carrizozo, New Mexico

Will Ed Harris, Director
Carrizozo Chamber of Commerce
Carrizozo, New Mexico[194]

The war of words continued into May, but from this letter came the origins of the special committee known as "The Friends of Billy the Kid." Of all the representatives of that organization, Sargent emerged as the engine of the movement.

Joe Owens Sargent was the "brains of the business." He was a slight man who sported horn-rimmed glasses. Beneath the spectacles, there was an undeniable spirit and affability. From his appearance, Sargent was a cross between a college professor and a cowboy. When he arrived in Carrizozo, the county seat of Lincoln County, he imbibed the area's legendary history. Since he was a businessman by nature, he quickly eased into a prominent position as president of the Chamber of Commerce.[195]

Sargent was born in January 1921 in Hale County, Texas. His father, Andrew Green Sargent, was a rooming house manager in Plainview, a town halfway between Lubbock and Amarillo. There were accounts about the Kid's presence in the region, and Joe grew up on the local lore. He married young, fathered several children, and divorced. Single again, he moved to Carrizozo, some twenty miles from Lincoln, near family and employment. Joe spied an opportunity when he purchased a building that housed both a bar and restaurant from his brother. The establishment known as the Yucca Bar positioned Joe Sargent at the center of Carrizozo's social life at the time. He was assisted greatly by his second wife Sharon, who he met while visiting California and married in 1953.[196]

The town prospered as a railroad stop near several military installations. Local legend provided the extra "zo" was added to distinguish the hamlet from another town named "Carrizo." Longtime resident Johnson Stearns wrote that businesses emerged astride the tracks by 1899. The growth was so phenomenal that, in 1913, Carrizozo became the county seat after an inter-county scrum with the old mining town of White Oaks. Ultimately, the decision was made by the U.S. Supreme Court.[197]

Outside Carrizozo and Lincoln County, Sargent gathered powerful allies for the cause of the Kid's return. One of the most influential voices was 59-year-old Alan Hinman Rhodes, the son of the famous author Eugene Manlove Rhodes. Although his father lived in and wrote stories of Billy the Kid's New Mexico, he passed away in 1934. Alan experienced the ranch life in his youth, but later removed to his parent's eastern home in Apalachin, New York. However, he and his mother May stayed connected to their former state of residence through their annual pilgrimages to Eugene Rhodes' grave near Alamogordo. They occasionally visited old friends in Carrizozo on occasion. Most importantly, Alan Rhodes knew Lois Telfer and influenced her decision to support the movement.[198]

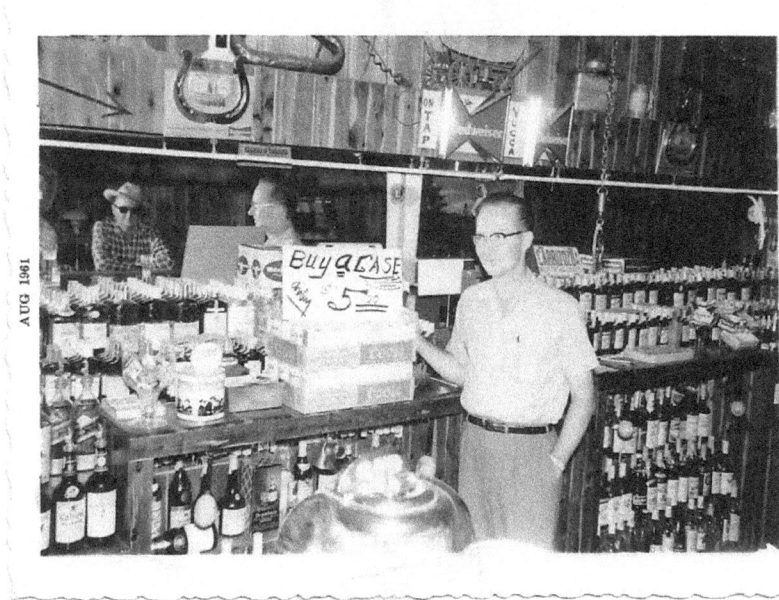

Joe Sargent at the Yucca Bar, Carrizozo, New Mexico, 1961. He was the undisputed leader of the "Friends of Billy the Kid."
Courtesy of Sharon Degner.

As representatives of the two counties sparred over the issue, the Lincoln County petitioners publicized Telfer's support for the return of the Kid's body in the press. She stated several people contacted her about the April 14th news story. Alan Rhodes and Roselle Rader, a descendant of the famous vanished editor and lawyer Colonel Albert Fountain, communicated with Telfer at the time. They co-wrote a letter, signed by Sargent and Lloyd Davis, a civic leader and developer at the resort community of Ruidoso, under the group's chosen name, "The Friends of Billy the Kid." It was published in full in the April 28, 1961 edition of the *Lincoln County News*.[199]

Dear Miss Telfor [sic]:

A group of people in Lincoln County have been considering the feasibility of re-interring the remains of Billy the Kid at Lincoln, which we consider his   rightful resting place. Enclosed you will find a copy of a letter to that effect written by the chairman of the Board of Lincoln County Commissioners to the board of DeBaca County Commissioners. Their answer to this request is "No."

Since this action has been taken, we have learned that you are his only known living relative. We respectfully seek your permission to accomplishing this aim, or perhaps you direct assistance, if needed.

As you know, Lincoln County is one of the most historical sections of the Southwest, and Billy the Kid, without doubt, is the most famous personality that ever pioneered the West. There are many people living in Lincoln County yet, who knew 'The Kid,' and the general feeling about him is more sympathetic than that of even

Pat Garrett. Therefore, we think that he should be re-interred at Lincoln. All expenses of this procedure will be paid by those of us who are interested in this project. Also, if this aim is accomplished, we have plans to create a park in Old Lincoln, memorializing the Lincoln County War, of which Billy was the principal participant, and his shrine would be a part thereof, according to your wishes. We anxiously await your reply (Signed.)[200]

The same issue of the *Lincoln County News* revealed Miss Telfer's response to the "Friends of Billy the Kid." Whatever she intended to infer, her response carried weight. In the limelight of publicity, Telfer unwisely ignored the bitter county tussle. As a young lady, she was used to occasional mention in the society pages of the Detroit newspaper. This was sparse experience, and it hardly prepared her for the intense public interest in her family connections. The paper announced Telfer's entire trip schedule.

She planned her arrival in El Paso, Texas about May 25, with a stay in Las Cruces before Memorial Day festivities in Lincoln.[201]

> *As a blood relative of Wm. H. Bonney (Billy the Kid), both being in direct descent from Thomas Bonney who came to America in 1634…may I offer any assistance to your request to have Billy's remains re-interred in Lincoln County.[202]*

The article poured gasoline on an open fire. The *Lincoln County News* published a warning from New Mexico State Senator M.P. Carr: *"If they start something like that we will take it to court…I don't blame them for trying, but we can't look at it that way."[203]* The news struck renewed fervor into some people, such as William Morrison, who a decade earlier championed "Brushy Bill" Roberts. On May 8, he typed a five-page letter to *Lincoln County News* publisher Paul Baker that not surprisingly reads like a case analysis.[204]

> *Mr Chester Chope of El Paso Herald Post had informed me that a report emanated in Ruidoso on the above styled subject [Re-interment, remains of Billy the Kid]. Then I read your editorial on April 14, Quote: "Let's settle this matter for all time," with which I agree from the standpoint of a historian.*
>
> *Of course, I cannot agree that re-interment of the remains of any, or all three buried there would accomplish this end. It was our intention to exhume the three and obtain anthropoligst [sic] reports to determine, which, if any, actually represented the cadaver of Kid. Also, we hoped to obtain ballistic reports in case of the Kid to determine whose pistol fired the lethal lead to accomplish the act.[205]*

Morrison veered off the subject of exhumation to air his personal suspicions on the coroner's report. Eventually he returned to the topic.

From the recent publicity you have given the subject, it is apparent that the Chairman of the Board of Lincoln County Commissioners has established the heirship of the Kid from Thomas Bonney, a common ancestor of Miss Lois H. Telfor [sic], who came to America in 1634; or that Miss Telfor [sic] can establish the fact that she is nearest of kin of Kid...

Of course, the burden of proof of death of Kid and proof of heirship of Miss Telfor [sic] falls on the moving party—in this case it is the Lincoln County Commissioners.[206]

Morrison's intent was revealed in the third page of the letter. He proposed his alliance to the exhumation in order to further his own work on "Brushy Bill" and the coroner's report. Morrison felt the exhumation <u>alone</u> would not settle the issue of the Kid's identity. However, the "Friends of Billy the Kid" had limited aims. Ever insistent in his beliefs, Morrison never separated the two different goals, which frustrated him.

However, after the establishment of these issues through court proceedings, I may be willing to enter into negotiations with them to defray all costs of proving heirship of O'Folliard and Bowdre; obtaining permission from their nearest of kin to exhume and re-inter all three in a location to be designated by them. Provided, however, that permission be granted to me to continue my scientific investigation as previously outlined herein.[207]

In effect, the publicity of the Morrison letter worsened the situation for the "Friends of Billy the Kid." It provided their adversaries with a blueprint to add Morrison's personal mission to the Lincoln County group. He handed the state's attorney an idea he later used in legal proceedings. In addition, Morrison circulated copies of his letter to "Honorable Harry S. Truman, Honorable John Ben Shepperd, Mr. Chester Chope, Senators I.M. Smalley and M.P. Carr."[208]

Far from the wide goals of Morrison, the "Friends" in Lincoln County kept a small circle. They preferred collaboration in local establishments. Artist John Meigs was a good friend of Joe Sargent and a frequent patron of the Yucca Bar. Sparked by Joe's historical mission, Meigs made his own impact on one of the Yucca's walls. Joe's wife Sharon remembered the large, colorful mural of Billy the Kid as an admired community landmark. The unanimously positive descriptions of the work ranged from its color to Meigs' depiction of the Kid.[209]

The Meigs mural at the Yucca Bar was inspired from a similar work from his mentor Peter Hurd. Hurd's opus with Billy the Kid as his subject was a 21 by 37-inch egg tempura piece entitled "The [Last] Escape of Billy the Kid." This unforgettable image portrayed a solitary Billy the Kid on horseback looking back at a distant storm brewing behind him. Ironically, Hurd's commission for that piece was in Lubbock, Texas, rather than either Lincoln or De Baca Counties in New Mexico. The location of Sargent's boyhood home allowed him greater access to this work. Interestingly, the plans of both Meigs and Sargent were perfectly aligned.[210]

Meigs was not the only prominent supporter of Sargent's activity. Helena LaMay and her cousin Mayme Coe Perry represented their family. Paul Almer Blazer, Sr., whose family owned the famous mill, and the occupational successor to Pat Garrett, Sheriff Glenn Bradley, were both in the group. Descendants of the Kid's Spanish allies were involved. Marguerite Salazar

Bernardo and Rufina Montoya Maes both had personal connections to the Kid himself. They were daughters of the Kid's best friend and the ally who aided his escape from Lincoln. Rhodes and Baker were already on board. Though a conditional member, Morrison was helpful during the formation period. He had paralegal experience, and he suggested that the Lincoln County commissioners research necessary legal records. They needed an attorney for their forthcoming plans.[211]

Bookplate of John L. Meigs. The artist and architect involved himself with several legacy projects on Billy the Kid.
Author's Collection.

Clarence C. Chase, Jr. was a young Alamogordo attorney who fit perfectly in with their plans. He was the grandson of one of New Mexico's most influential and infamous men, Albert Bacon Fall.

His grandfather served as U.S. President Warren G. Harding's interior secretary from March 1921 to March 1923. While in this position, he was accused of steering public oil leases to his friend's companies. The "Teapot Dome" scandal landed Fall for a stint in jail, but the family remained a political force in New Mexico. The handsome, well-groomed "C.C." had a trim moustache that accentuated his class. Like his grandfather, he flirted with politics. However, by the summer of 1961, the 37-year-old attorney was hired to regain Billy the Kid's body for Lincoln County.[212]

Lois Telfer's second visit to New Mexico bolstered the Lincoln County movement. Proof was found on invitations to a May 30, 1961 luncheon at Lincoln's Wortley Hotel. The printed invitation cards went out to the "Friends of Billy the Kid." In bold print, the card read:

You are cordially invited to a RECEPTION honoring Miss Lois Telfer of New York City (Only surviving relative of Billy the Kid) at the Wortley Hotel in Lincoln, New Mexico promptly at 10:00 A.M., May 30 Luncheon following[213]

One had a handwritten note scrawled in cursive writing. It said: *"The business of re-interring 'Billy the Kid' in Old Lincoln will be discussed."*[214]

On the evening of May 25, Lois Telfer arrived at El Paso International Airport, and greeted by Joe Sargent and a host of news reporters. Most of them tried to get a quote on her way to a reception at the Hilton. The simmering battle with De Baca County remained in the scribe's stories, and the drama of Telfer's visit heightened with each mention of it. A quote of "no surrender" from Chairman Colter and mentions of Morrison's involvement easily found places in print. The Wortley Hotel meeting was the epicenter of the visit, and the newsprint hyped it appropriately.[215]

Publisher Baker of the *Lincoln County News* positioned Telfer's visit on its front page, and published Colter's latest missive in full for effect. Withheld for a time, the response was actually from Lincoln County's May 8 letter. The Commissioner invited them to visit Fort Sumner. It read in part:

Considering the glories of the past it is not surprising that every man, woman and child in De Baca County is fully aware of the historical events which took place here. We do not need artificial means, such as pageants, to stimulate interest in our history. The residents of this county live in and with their history and would be embarrassed if it were necessary to have special events, timed during the tourist season, to recall the past.

We would be happy to have any and all of your people in Lincoln County visit our county so that they could become aware of its historical significance. We would not set a date for your visit as you are welcome in De Baca County at any time and any of our citizens will be glad to act as hosts and guides. It should be an informative and valuable experience of your citizens to come in contact with another, and we think better, approach to history.

In your letters to us there have been many references to the "relatives of Billy the Kid." We have carefully consulted the history books and all the old-timers in the area and they are unanimous in stating that William H. Bonney, alias Billy the Kid, was never married. If there are residents of Lincoln County who claim descent from Billy the Kid, the evidence proving this should, we think, be made public. Surely Lincoln County would not keep secret any facts which relate this most notable citizen.[216]

Baker answered Colter's pointed communication with his own editorial. He emphasized the Commissioner's retort towards the pageant, riled up the prideful scions of Lincoln. He wrote in part:

De Baca County is suddenly finding itself on the defensive in resisting Lincoln County's move to re-inter the remains of Billy the Kid in a memorial park at Lincoln; however, they have not retreated from their stand that any exploitation of the Kid's grave at Fort Sumner is purely coincidental, and even if it were not, he was nothing but a common outlaw.

Lincoln County has challenged this label as unjust on several grounds, two of which are that the Kid had more friends than enemies and that he had been offered amnesty by the Government of the United States and Territory of New Mexico.

Lincoln County proposes to re-inter Billy the Kid in a suitable shrine at Lincoln, New Mexico, near the final scenes of the Lincoln County War and the Last Escape. Surely De Baca county, which has only words of ridicule and contempt for the Kid will not continue to refuse this reasonable request of its neighboring county.

The people of De Baca County are to be congratulated in having such a profound sense of history that nothing like a pageant is needed to recall past glories of the county. Texans should heed this and close up the Alamo; likewise the Custer battlefield, Gettysburg, and other shrines.[217]

Baker's editorial emphasized the battle lines that divided Lincoln and De Baca Counties at Lois Telfer's arrival. Still, she noticed little as she fulfilled her itinerary. When she checked in at the Amador Hotel in Las Cruces, Telfer secretly met Pat Garrett's youngest daughter Pauline. Unlike the contentious meeting between her brother Oscar and "Brushy Bill" a decade before, the visit was cordial. Telfer described her as "a fine girl," who spent a career as assistant to the Dona Ana County school superintendent. They were both single women, but Pauline raised five of her siblings' children as her own. Neither publicized the meeting, and it was kept out of the newspapers. Telfer confessed it to Mullin in correspondence months later.[218]

Nearly as secretive as Telfer's meeting with Pauline Garrett was her stay with Elizabeth Fountain Armendariz in nearby Mesilla. She was the daughter of lawyer and newspaper man Col. Albert J. Fountain, the former defense attorney for Billy the Kid in 1881. According to Telfer, Fountain was "confident to acquit him" had he not been killed. In 1896, the Colonel disappeared on the White Sands with his young son Henry, but his other children carried on his legacy. Elizabeth married Auveliano Armendariz, a musician born in Chihuahua, Mexico. The couple threw a party in Telfer's honor, and the dancing ensued. *"Aunt Elizabeth [Armendariz],"* Telfer proclaimed, *"is the most wonderful woman. We had mariachi singers and dancing and everything at her home. It was wonderful."*[219]

Telfer returned to Lincoln County and the anticipated meeting with the "Friends of Billy the Kid." After a Sunday reception at the Carrizozo Chamber of Commerce, she had little time before the well-attended reception at the Wortley Hotel on Tuesday, May 30. The considerable news coverage included a piece from El Paso reporter Bill McGaw. The first line of his article foreshadowed the coming tension. McGaw wrote the *"bones of Billy the Kid may rise again soon to stir up another Lincoln County War—this one perhaps not so bloody as the original, but every bit as bitter."*[220]

McGaw was not disappointed. The Wortley luncheon was a high-spirited affair that evoked memories of a high-school pep rally. Sargent was in charge, but there was no shortage of speakers during the course of the discussion. Wilbur Coe declared the Kid was actually not an outlaw, but a "victim of circumstance." He drew loud applause when he said that the Kid's "bones belong in his hometown."[221] Furthermore, he extolled the benefits of increased tourism to both De Baca and Lincoln Counties. There was an official announcement for Chase to arrange the legal details. With

Telfer's proclaimed status as the only living relative of Billy the Kid, the lawyer expected a fight from De Baca County. Chase stated if they lost their fight in the state's district court, they planned to push the case all the way to the New Mexico State Supreme Court. Alan Rhodes, who drove from his New York home to attend, pledged his support "in any manner." Margaret Salazar Bernardo spoke of her adopted father Yginio and his close friendship with the Kid. As the only girl in her family, Yginio doted on her and related stories few knew about. 80-year-old Rufina Maes, the daughter of the Kid's opponent Lucio Montoya, was in concert with the others on their goals. Helena LaMay endorsed the tourism benefit, as this alone made the project worth the effort. Her first cousin Mayme Coe Perry, whose father George Coe was author of the book *Frontier Fighter*, contemplated a reprint after a compliment from Rhodes.[222]

The Wortley Hotel luncheon revealed the realities of a coming fight for the body of Billy the Kid. Lincoln County Sheriff Glenn Bradley was a former politician in the state legislature, and he warned the group might be in need of his services. Paul Blazer favored the return of the Kid's body, but preferred more discussion on positive topics. Chase admitted that success depended on Ms. Telfer's evidence of kinship. With this, Telfer gave a detailed speech about her family's knowledge of the Kid. While still a child, her Great-Grandmother Judith Bonney revealed the relationship to her. Although her parents never discussed it with her, she said there was ample documentation. No one in the room dissented from the plan. Even the operators of the hotel in attendance, the preservationists John and Nan Boylan, seemed positive over its prospects. After the meeting ended, Mrs. LaMay and Ms. Telfer visited with Ramon Maes and his personal exhibit of artifacts before departing for another of the Kid's frequenting places, the ghost town of White Oaks.[223]

The high-profile "Friends of Billy the Kid" luncheon at the Wortley heightened both expectations and tensions between the two counties. On June 2, Baker published a front-page story in the *Lincoln County News*. The sensational headline "Excitement grows over Billy's body" was published alongside a lengthy piece penned by Morrison. A poem entitled "A Ballad of Lonely Bill" was included. The largest space was dedicated to Telfer's doings in Lincoln and a vote on the reburial issue. Baker reported the result was unanimous in favor of the move. After the vote, *"[Lincoln County] Sheriff W.G. Bradley noted that he had a gun and was willing to use it on any "nay" voters."*[224]

A new phase began in the battle for the body of Billy the Kid. With clear battle lines drawn, the threshold was crossed. A press-based war of words developed into a legal struggle bound for the courtroom. Both sides appeared to be "all in" for their respective causes. The "push and pull" of a mocking rivalry became a nasty legal scrum. It was only a short time before legal papers found their way to a judge.

CHAPTER FIVE

THE PETITION

By June 1961, two New Mexico counties declared war on each other for the dead corpse of the famed outlaw Billy the Kid. A group of citizens and local officials in Lincoln County faced hostility from officials and public opinion in De Baca County. The latter had the body in its boundaries, and the former wanted possession. Over the following nine months, attorneys battled in the courts and newspapers, bringing mocking comparisons to the Lincoln County War—when the Kid was alive. Similar to the ugly print exchanges during the Kid's day, the *Lincoln County News* and the *De Baca County News* published the frenzied events with plenty of nasty rhetoric over relocating the Kid's remains. The Lincoln County contingent had fancy ammunition with Lois Telfer. Without her, the fight between De Baca and Lincoln Counties would lose impetus. Telfer brought clout and national press attention to Lincoln County's cause.[225]

Regional newspapers followed the proclaimed "last surviving relative of Billy the Kid." The redheaded New Yorker publicized her disappointment in Fort Sumner through her summer 1959 visit. The press story recalled the full import of Telfer's disappointment after she purchased a wreath for her relative's grave. Once on the grounds of the Old Fort Cemetery, Telfer found a wire fence barred entry to the cemetery. Frustrated, she tossed the wreath over the barrier. It landed just inside the grounds, far from the Kid's memorial. A national audience witnessed Lois Telfer's disappointment all over again.[226]

Telfer returned to Fort Sumner in the summer of 1960, again determined to visit the grave of Billy the Kid. From her bus, she viewed the highway billboards advertising the Kid's burial place. The sight bothered her. Fort Sumner operated a cottage tourist industry around the death of her relative. On this second visit, she approached a building bordering the cemetery. Upon close inspection, her fears were confirmed. The graveyard was in rough shape, although an attractive memorial marker for the Kid and his two allies commanded public attention. A group of tombstones, the final resting places of the Maxwell family, graced one corner of the cemetery. The widowed owner of the property, Mrs. Helene Allen, paid no attention to her. She interacted with a group of tourists, which annoyed Telfer. Her subsequent discussion with the owner only deteriorated the situation. Mrs. Allen was offended by Telfer's suggestions to improve cemetery conditions. Likewise, her tourists ignored her. Additionally, the reception was peppered with uttered doubts about her lineage.[227]

The bad experiences at the Old Fort Cemetery bolstered Telfer's resolve to move the body of Billy the Kid, but detractors of the project were not limited to De Baca County representatives. Some Lincoln County War historians viewed it negatively. Philip Rasch kept his distance from the "Friends of Billy the Kid." He wrote to Sonnichsen on June 5,

I really can't get too sympathetic with those who wish to move the Kid's body to Lincoln. After 80 years this sudden interest leaves me cold. But I must confess that I should like to see the grave opened. I have always wondered a little bit about these stories that the Kid's body was stolen shortly after burial. [Pat] Garrett flatly denied it, of course, but ----I wonder.[228]

Rasch referred to one of several historical rumors. The first involved a possible removal of the Kid's body when the remains of soldiers were transferred from the Old Fort site to a national cemetery in Albuquerque. The second, from the 1930s account from cowboy-turned-politician Jack Potter, claimed that previous landowners removed the Kid's wooden cemetery marker as a souvenir. Finally, floods obscured the true locations of most graves at the Old Fort Cemetery. By 1961, few people with first-hand knowledge of the Kid's burial spot remained.[229]

In 1961, there was some documentation of grave locations. An engineer's map was drawn by Charles W. Burrow of Santa Fe, who surveyed the grounds for the military interments. Although rudimentary, the map provided some guidance. Burrow's hand-drawn map contained 30 numbered graves and reference to unknown civilian burial locations. In addition, Burrow wrote personal notes. One stated *"some civilians buried between old adobe wall and wire fence."* Number 28 was *"Billy the Kid,"* next to two *"members of the Kid's Gang."* These referenced the burial sites of Charlie Bowdre and Tom O'Folliard. They were not aligned alongside each other. One grave was set back a row from the other.[230]

Burrow's map of the Old Fort Cemetery had a curious feature. Two lines measured space between the Kid's grave and that of two others—an *"unknown child"* and *"child of Bobien [sic] family."* There was no explanation on the map, but the two children were in close proximity to their kinsmen in the Maxwell and Beaubien Families, the original owners of the land grant. The monument honoring the Kid, Bowdre, and O'Folliard collectively as "Pals" was placed in a central location to all three graves. Eventually, a concrete walk made access easier. According to one Old Fort

Museum docent, the current walk is literally over one of the three bodies.[231]

As tensions elevated between the two counties, it was only a matter of time before the legal action started. Chase would file papers in De Baca County against "two parties." Lois Telfer left for New York after *"a week here formulating plans for removal of the body"*[232] Chase wondered aloud in print about the impartiality of any deciding judge in De Baca County. He said, *"In my opinion, neither the judges in this district or that (De Baca County) should rule on it, as it will cause anamosity[sic]."*[233] For any other judicial appointment, a "Writ of Mandamus" was needed to confer on lower courts. In other words, Chase displayed his intended legal strategy in public.

For several weeks, there was no word on the petition. Still, there was discussion among historians. Robert Mullin wrote Leland Sonnichsen from California on June 23, acknowledging the press clip of Telfer's visit. Although her claims as the Kid's relative were strong, he demurred from their reburial plans. He stated, *"She wrote me about the Lincoln affair and asked me to meet her there, but of course that was impractical."*[234] Nonetheless, the historian thought kindly of her. Mullin visited New York to *"meet her friends in Greenwich Villiage [sic]; she is (or was) one of the most brilliantly illuminated persons with whom I ever appeared in public; her hair was dyed a brilliant orange—with costume to match. This makes her sound like a wild woman, but as a matter of fact she is a very pleasant, nice person."*[235]

De Baca County did not share Mullin's favorable opinion of Lois Telfer, particularly once legal maneuvers began. On June 26, the long-awaited petition was recorded in the civil docket of the 10th Judicial District Court. "In Re Application of Lois Telfer, Petitioner, For the Removal of the Body of William H. Bonney,

Deceased, From the Fort Sumner Cemetery in Which He [sic] is interred for Re-interrment in the Lincoln, New Mexico, Cemetery" was filed as No. 3255. The defendants were the Board of County Commissioners and Mrs. J.W. Allen. The petition was four typewritten pages with twelve numbered points. At the end was a sworn statement signed by Telfer on June 8th. De Baca County Clerk Judy Marshall issued the summons for Sheriff James W. Hopper, and he in turn served the same on both defendant parties the same day.[236]

In the twelve points, chief among them was Lois Telfer's standing as the "next of kin" to Billy the Kid; that after the fort's abandonment, "care and control" of the cemetery fell to De Baca County's commissioners; that the cemetery was "for all intents and purposes" abandoned without a burial in the preceding five years; that the De Baca County Board of County Commissioners would not relinquish control of the body; and that Mrs. Allen claimed interest in the property.[237]

The newspapers wrote about the court filing in short order. On June 27, a news story entitled "Outlaw's Grave Feud Rages" outlined the issues. It further deepened the divide between the two counties by reporting that Lois Telfer sought a restraining order for Mrs. Allen and the De Baca County Commission from interfering with the process.[238] This was verified in an *El Paso Herald-Post* article three days later.

Filing of a court action in an attempt to remove the Kid's body from its grave seven miles southeast of here for reburial in Lincoln County has aroused feelings of bitterness, contempt, skepticism and puzzlement among residents of Fort Sumner. The attempt to remove the Kid's body offers some interesting possibilities...which may result in little short of a shooting war if some one [sic] starts digging around in the old graveyard.[239]

De Baca County residents felt the suit was incorrectly filed. The burial ground was public domain after a judgement from the U.S. Court in Denver. As Mrs. Allen did not own the cemetery, the Commissioners likewise felt relieved of the responsibility. She explained that her late husband purchased the land enveloping the cemetery, but she was prevented from her attempts to maintain it from "irate relatives of persons buried there."[240]

While there were a number of valid points in the June 30th *El Paso Herald Post* article, there was also ill-advised quotes. Commissioners vowed to "keep the body" in defiance to Lincoln's overtures, yet gave weak excuses for their lack of maintenance of the burial ground. Indeed, court activity probably delayed the Allens in cleaning up the property, but the community profited as well. Residents were appalled at "outsiders" coming into Fort Sumner and dictating terms of maintenance to them. However, De Baca County could have avoided the entire mess through public maintenance. The article made some important points in favor of De Baca County as well. The possibility of entire families placed in small unmarked plots, the Kid's missing marker and the faded memories of older residents raised too many questions to locate the Kid's body.[241]

Neither side compromised in the intensifying print war. The headline of the Friday, June 30, 1961 *Milwaukee Journal Green Sheet* declared: "Two New Mexico Towns fight for the Remains of Billy the Kid." Pithy statements from Sheriff Bradley and Morrison peppered the story, which was picked up by other publications nationwide. Bradley vowed to bring back the Kid—dead, not alive. Morrison planned to furnish documents from his research, and reiterated his quest for a pardon of the Kid. De Baca County officials repeated its oft-used defense and asked why Lincoln County waited eighty years.[242]

In truth, some in Lincoln County felt divided in their sentiment after the petition was filed. Members of the Old Lincoln County Memorial Commission, only months away from their trademark event of the summer season, the annual pageant, competed for newsprint space. John Boylan, in his position as curator of the Lincoln County Courthouse, announced that television stuntman Bob Bickston would assist with that summer's version, planned for August 4-6. In Boylan's announcement, there was no mention of the lawsuit or the removal of the Kid's body. This was no accidental omission. As made evident in later writings, the Boylans opposed the removal, and few others in the Commission championed a fight with De Baca County.[243]

Despite a division of opinion for the movement of the Kid in Lincoln, the biggest obstacle was time. Tourist season was ripe at the time the petition was filed, and the wait for a formal hearing lingered for months. In the meantime, there was plenty of time for the two counties to inflict wounds on each other. The constant news flow didn't help. On July 5, the *Arizona Republic* reported that it "may be difficult" to identify the Kid's body, as all three of the Regulators died about the same age. "A pathologist or anthropologist" would be challenged. The article stated that little care about the body was found.[244] The *De Baca County News* responded by publishing an editorial denoting the cruelty of disturbing graves, and it claimed Lincoln County never wanted his remains back until then. Never passing on an opportunity, Baker's *Lincoln County News* reprinted the editorial.[245]

While the newspapers stayed busy, the attorneys worked feverishly as well. Assistant District Attorney for the Tenth District

John Humphrey, Jr. did his homework. A local lawyer from nearby Clovis, his daughter Myrl Jane related his background. As a young man he overcame hepatitis to study law at Harvard University. While his father wanted him to stay in New Mexico and his established milk route, his mother dutifully stepped in for him. He was a true history buff who personally knew the local descendants of the Maxwell family. When the petition was filed, he knew what that meant for the economic health of his region.[246]

The July 5 story went nationwide, and the result was a plot twist for the ages. The story published in the *Tulsa World* reached a postal service worker in Bartlesville, Oklahoma named Louis Bowdre. Upset by the news of the petition, he immediately wrote the district court a strong objection to move the Kid's body. *"I am hereby protesting such action. My cousin, "Charlie Bowdre," is buried beside Billy...Although I'm not particularly proud of Charlie's nefarious activities, he was a member of our family and I would prefer to let well enough alone."*[247]

Louis Allen Bowdre, Sr. was an interesting man who dedicated his life to public service. He was born on December 2, 1917 in Meeker, Oklahoma. He grew up in Osage County, enlisted in the military in 1936, and served throughout World War II, reaching the rank of sergeant with the 77th Field Artillery. He was wounded at the Battle of the Bulge in January 1945 and received numerous medals for his military service. He married in 1941 and started a family. Bowdre started with the Postal Service at the Stillwater office, but moved to Bartlesville in 1954. His daughter Sue Tennell noted his interest in the Old West, and the story of the Kid astounded him.[248]

The announcement from Louis Bowdre arrived as Humphrey planned a filing to dismiss Lois Telfer's petition on July 18. Humphrey laid out four points: a failure to state a claim which relief could be granted; failure to state proper defendants for said relief; that relatives are "indispensable parties"; and that the cemetery was public property. Humphrey's daughter confirmed that her father had contacted Bowdre. It was a solid strategy by pitting one descendant against the will of another, but the legal maneuvering was far from finished.[249]

Chase delivered the next salvo. The assigned district judge for the hearing, Jacobo Vincent (J.V.) Gallegos of Tucumcari, New Mexico, was personally close to District Attorney Victor Breen, Humphrey's direct supervisor. The relationship was well known, and Chase lost no time in filing an affidavit of disqualification against the judge. On July 25, the move parried Humphrey's dismissal paperwork. Clerk Judy Marshall announced that both sides disagreed on the presiding official, and New Mexico's Supreme Court would appoint a new judge. Two days later, the order was signed designating Judge Elias T. Hensley, Jr., of the Ninth District, as the new presiding official in Case Number 3255.[250]

The move by Chase and the "Friends of Billy the Kid" kept the petition case alive and ensured a protracted court battle. When the judicial change was published in the August 3 *Lincoln County News*, the Lincoln Pageant was in full swing. The owners of Carrizozo's Hampton-Holland Funeral Home, Steve Hampton and H.K. Holland, published an open letter to the "Friends of Billy the Kid" to remove and rebury the remains "without fee."[251] They required written permission from Telfer and the proper ruling from the courts, but they made the offer *"with no intent of personal publicity, but a deep-seated conviction that Billy the Kid was and is one of the most misunderstood and maligned gunfighters of the old west and deserves the decent treatment..."*[252]

Throughout the summer of 1961, news of the court proceedings loomed. With no sign of a new court date, an informational vacuum developed. Meanwhile, Lois Telfer enjoyed support in New York. Telfer's good friend Sylvester Vigilante was on a "hot trail" that he intended to follow up. She noted the proof of her relationship with the Kid was in her records. Mullin, recovering from an illness, briefly re-entered the fray in mid-August. Hearing of the court action, Mullin wrote Telfer, who responded in a letter from New York dated August 16. She replied with her usual gusto.[253]

I did <u>not</u> start the issue for Billy's removal. A large group, "Friends of Billy the Kid," headed by Joe Sargent, Mayor Ball of Carizozo, Sheriff Glen Bradley (the present Pat Garrett) & the most prominent cattlemen of Lincoln Co. did this. I hate publicity, but at the urging of Alan Rhodes, (son of Eugene Manlove) & Helena Coe La May (Frank Coe's daughter) who says "They are Right as Rain," I offered to help, & we are going to fight to a finish. Mullin, if you had seen all those fine citizens (over 200) in the Lincoln Court room on May 30 including all that[']s left of the blood relatives of the original participants, you would realize what this means to them.[254]

Perhaps the biggest revelation of the August 16 letter came at the end of the five-page letter. Telfer admitted to Mullin that she visited with Pat Garrett's daughter Pauline in Las Cruces. She asked Mullin not to relate her meeting with Pauline Garrett to anyone, and wrote Mullin that "W.A.K."[William A. Keleher] sent her a letter wishing her success. Again, she warned the historian to not relate that piece of news.[255] The secretive nature of the conversation with Pauline Garrett was important. If supported by a Garrett family member, the petitioners had access to possible knowledge that helped their legal arguments, such as whether there were proper burial papers filed by her father. Although out of character for Mullin to break a confidence, he regularly wrote other historians, including Keleher. In other words, confidences were not assured.[256]

Good friends Lois Telfer, right, and Helena Coe LaMay, 1960.
Courtesy of Nellie Ruth Jones.

The petition movement crested in August 1961. The successful disqualification of Judge Gallegos proved the "Friends of Billy the Kid" had widespread support. With volunteers in tow, the petitioners tasted success in their initial endeavors. The Pageant was over, and Billy the Kid's name was fresh in everyone's mind thanks to constant news coverage. Only misfortune stood between them and the eventual hearing.

Tragedy struck in the morning hours of Saturday, August 21, 1961. At about 9 a.m., Joe and Sharon Sargent were just getting ready for their day. In July 2013, Sharon described what happened at their residence.

It was about nine o'clock in the morning and I was getting ready to go to work at the bar. Joe was in bed, asleep and all the air conditioning [unit] fell on his head...I had a mirror from the floor to the ceiling, and I was standing putting my makeup on and getting dressed, and I could hear the mirror crackle...and I thought, 'What in the World?' And then about that time there was...a long hall from the closet into the dining room, and it [an explosion] threw me down this hall, and through an adobe wall...it just wasn't my time...[257]

A gas main ruptured, and the fissure literally blew apart the Sargent home. A large section of roof collapsed on top of Joe Sargent, pinning him underneath the rubble. Sharon was thrown clear, but only because the adobe wall crumbled. Dr. Aubrey N. (A.N.) Spencer, a regular customer at the Yucca Bar, rushed to the scene. Dick Butts, an off-duty soldier from the nearby Red Canyon installation, threw off large pieces of the wall to reach the helpless Sargent. At first glance, it appeared the wounds were limited to a broken leg. He stayed awake for the first minutes, but soon slipped into unconsciousness.[258]

Joe Sargent never recovered from the blast. The leg wound was seen to the eye, but the trauma to his skull and internal hemorrhaging was not. He clung to life for seven days, but never opened his eyes again. On Saturday, August 28, 1961, Joe Sargent passed away at the age of 40. Sharon Sargent's stay in the hospital lasted nearly a month. When recovered, she thanked those citizens who assisted them in the rescue efforts following the explosion. However, she prepared for a long recuperation.[259]

Recuperation was not possible for the "Friends of Billy the Kid." The timing could not have been worse. Additionally, the removal of the movement's energetic leader weighted the shoulders of Chase and Telfer. As soon as Sargent's casket was lowered in Carrizozo's Evergreen Cemetery, the chance of reburying Billy the Kid in Lincoln County was reduced. Chase could lead in court, but not keep the organization intact. The only hope to energize the petition movement was another appearance from Lois Telfer.[260]

The fiery New Yorker penned Mullin a letter dated October 23 with her reaction to Sargent's death. *"My case is postponed so far, as Joe Sargent to whom I gave power of atty. to represent me, had a bad explosion in his house in Carrizozo. He died a week later. Chase writes that he will continue as usual. I have complete confidence in C.C. Chase."*[261] In the same letter, she lashed out at Phillip Rasch, who sent a contrarian opinion on the case to the *Lincoln County News* and angered the "Friends." Telfer felt Rasch was two-faced for writing her "syrupcy" [sic] letters that praised her ancestor, but thought he turned against her after a perceived snub on the Wortley luncheon in May. Telfer had no role in the invitations, but Rasch did himself few favors for his aggressive behavior that bordered on rudeness. In fact, an uninvited visit to Helena LaMay in a Carrizozo hospital room may have been the reason.[262]

There was scheduled legal activity in late November, when an answer to the petition was expected. In preparation, Helena LaMay wrote Morrison that she was staying with her daughter in Roswell during the winter months. Chase was busy planning their legal strategy. Telfer continued to write friends and press contacts from

New York. Despite the loss of Joe Sargent, all believed they would prevail. Like the suddenness of Sargent's death, another development blocked their ambitions to rebury the body of Billy the Kid.[263]

CHAPTER SIX

THE INTERVENOR

In autumn 1961, the pending case to remove the body of Billy the Kid from the Old Fort Cemetery at Fort Sumner was tense for both sides. The petition filed the previous summer, the removal of a judge, and the death of Joe Sargent ensured drama. For several months, everything was on hold. The aforementioned events brought news stories, heated rhetoric, and another surprise. A familiar name from the past entered the case: Charlie Bowdre.

Bartlesville, Oklahoma resident Louis Allen Bowdre represented family interests for Billy the Kid's burial companion. He was introduced through an opinion piece published in regional newspapers in July. Most took little notice at the time as Bowdre was far from New Mexico. Assistant District Attorney John Humphrey, Jr. changed that perception by involving Louis Bowdre in the case as an official intervenor. The postal worker brought Charlie Bowdre directly into the case. The Lincoln County group had Lois Telfer's persistent claims of proof to a solid family relationship to Billy the Kid. That alone convinced them of eventual victory.[264]

Charlie Bowdre's closest family members actually lived in Arkansas, Mississippi, and Texas. The family moved into these sections of the country from their native Mississippi about the same time Charlie fought alongside the Kid. Charlie's younger brother Benjamin Thomas, known as Benjamin, moved to the small hamlet of Plumerville, Arkansas, approximately 45 miles west of Little Rock. The family prospered as merchants, and in time, Plumerville boasted Bowdre Street as one of its main thoroughfares. He married a young woman named Noda Hull and fathered three children: Paul, Esther, and Elizabeth. Most of his family keepsakes, including a valuable image of Charlie and most of the Kid's gang, passed through this family. Benjamin died in Plumerville on November 20, 1913. Some of Charlie's siblings resided in Hernando, Mississippi, not far from the family birthplace. In autumn 1961, there were numerous relatives in the Bowdre family available if Humphrey sought them.[265]

In addition, possible intervenors already lived in New Mexico. When Charlie Bowdre's widow Manucla died at San Patricio in February 1939, she had numerous children from her three subsequent marriages. Undoubtedly, they knew about the adventures of Charlie Bowdre and the Kid through their mother. Unlike the hushed whispers of the Bowdre family, the Spanish families recounted the accounts of the Regulators for posterity. This was evident through the numerous interviews undertaken throughout the 1930s as part of President Franklin D. Roosevelt's Works Progress Administration (WPA) and several books by former New Mexico Governor Miguel Antonio Otero. Yet, there is no indication that Humphrey sought their testimony.[266]

There was a legitimate explanation for the abbreviated search of the Bowdre family for intervenors in the case. Humphrey's limited preparation time for court, coupled with Louis Bowdre's willingness to file a motion to intervene, convinced the lawyer that no further inquiry was necessary. The old postman planned to travel from his Oklahoma home for the hearing, but hindsight proved a diligent search for closer relations was needed. However, it's hard to fault the Assistant District Attorney for overlooking "a bird in the hand." Amazingly, no record existed that Bowdre's close relatives even knew of the case or Louis Bowdre's role in it.[267]

The case returned to the De Baca County Courthouse with its new jurist. On November 9, 1961, the *Lincoln County News* announced a hearing on the 16th before District Judge Elias T. Hensley, Jr. The son of an Oklahoma medical examiner, Judge Hensley, 51, was raised in Portales, New Mexico and attended schools in Arkansas, Louisiana, and Wisconsin. He became district attorney for New Mexico's Ninth Judicial District in 1941, followed by an appointment as a district judge six years later. Judge Hensley was widely respected among the state's legal community, and the news comforted Humphrey in advance of the proceedings.[268]

On November 16, the opening salvo was Humphrey's immediate attempt to quash Lois Telfer's petition. In a motion filed by the attorneys and Mrs. Allen, they sought dismissal of the case based on the uncertainty of the grave location. The *Albuquerque Journal* reported that Humphrey stated that the memorial marker represented a "best guess" on the burial locations of the Kid and "his two friends."[269] Several witnesses testified at this initial hearing. Carlos F. Clancy, a resident of Albuquerque, recalled the Kid's unmarked grave when he visited before the flood. Luciano Frank, the grandson of Jesus Silva, admitted the disagreement on the location of the Kid's grave among three contemporaries. Fort Sumner mortician Walter Julian testified that "two or three tries" were made to locate a vacant plot during the last burial at the cemetery in 1946. Lincoln County's C.C. Chase parried this argument by questioning whether a detailed search for the correct location was considered near the agreed-upon grave. Julian admitted that no attempted search occurred "to his knowledge."[270]

The result of the November hearing was a draw. Witnesses spread uncertainty of the Kid's burial plot within the cemetery boundaries, but Chase extended the life of the case. None of the witnesses, he argued, proved no burial occurred "within 40 or 50 feet of the Kid's grave."[271] The De Baca County witnesses successfully claimed their ignorance of the exact location, but it was not enough to quash Telfer's petition. Judge Hensley overruled the motion from Humphrey and Allen, and he set the second hearing date for December 15th. It was a temporary setback for De Baca County interests.[272]

Within a week of Judge Hensley's decision, Humphrey moved on the first of several fronts. On the 22nd, he filed an "Answer to Petition." This document was composed of six points: the primary defense of the body's uncertain location, and five separate weaker arguments. The remainder of the document addressed the claims of the petition without any detailed comment. Some of the separate defenses included the 80-year time gap between the Kid's death and the petition and Telfer's distant relationship to the Kid. On this last point he wrote, *"...such relationship is so distant that petitioner has no standing to ask for the relief prayed for in her petition filed herein."*[273] A supporting statement declared that *"over the years, large numbers of persons have been buried"* and that any search for Bonney's body would result in *"disturbing the remains of numerous other persons buried in said cemetery."*[274] Lastly, Humphrey noted the prominent people buried in the cemetery made the grounds a historical site.[275]

In New York, Lois Telfer followed the court activity. She penned confidential letters to her friends. Although some of her communications were ill-advised, her resolve stayed firm. To Robert Mullin, who she referred to as "R.N.M.," Telfer admitted that Chase undertook *"a courageous fight, against tremendeous [sic] odds. His life, mine, & Joe Sargent's have been threatened more than once. Joe died a violent death, same week, he was to represent me in 1st Trial [sic]."*[276] Mullin read the newspapers, although his primary interest was in Telfer's relationship to the Kid.

He pressed her for more details about the Kid's surname of Bonney. It was likely Mullin was testing Telfer's credibility for himself.[277]

Other interested parties also read about the case. On December 1, Nan Boylan wrote historian and fellow Old Lincoln County Memorial Commission member William Keleher. The communication confirmed Mrs. Boylan's contrarian stance on the matter. Although the couple raised no objections at the Wortley Hotel luncheon in May, she claimed that *"in the Lincoln settlement, hostility to the plan is growing"* and visitors to the old courthouse who mentioned it *"are opposed to the plan 100%."*[278] Additionally, Mrs. Boylan admitted that she wrote Lois Telfer *"in a friendly manner, mentioning in passing, that hostility is spreading to this area."*[279] In reality, Mrs. Boylan feared repercussions from publicity that emanated from the suit and its effect on the Commission's work. If Telfer won the case, reburial in Lincoln directly involved the Commission. As support for her opinion, she polled local families and lobbied other members of the body. Boylan concluded a majority of the votes opposed the plan for reburial in Lincoln. She hoped for Keleher's support.[280]

Nan Boylan assumed much in her letter to William Keleher. She admitted intercession of her own accord with Telfer. In asking others to do so, she presumed the resulting pressure might prompt the New Yorker to close down her efforts for the Kid's body. She claimed the allegiance of four of her fellow commissioners, namely Mrs. Dessie Sawyer, Frank Kindel, Albert T. Pfingsten, and Col. Ewing Lusk, as opposed to the hearing. She *"counted five families who are for it (including the local bar owner [Ramon Maes] who is strongly for it); thirteen families who are against it (including seven of the town fathers who are vehemently opposed); and five families whose feelings in the matter I have not heard expressed."*[281] Apparently only visitors who discussed the matter with her were opposed to it, but that hardly meant every tourist in Lincoln felt likewise.[282]

On December 4, William Keleher responded to Mrs. Boylan. He wrote that about *"two years ago Miss Telfer talked to me about this matter and I did not encourage her at all...I doubt very much if anything can be accomplished by having the Commission disapprove the project or declare that the Commission will not furnish a grave site in Lincoln in the event the court authorizes the removal of the body."*[283] Keleher doubted Telfer would "pay attention" to Boylan's letter. However, he thought Mullin might assist her. In closing, he doubted the success of the case by the "Friends of Billy the Kid."[284]

Articles in the *Lincoln County News* seemed more jubilant about the possibilities of their success. On November 23, an article entitled "Billy's Future is Looking Brighter," practically claimed victory before that was possible. Chase was interviewed for the article. He *"said the defendants would have 10 days to file responsive pleadings, which they probably won't do, and then the going was clear to get to the heart of the matter—the petition for removal of Billy to Lincoln County."*[285] The news drove some to poetry, such as *Roswell Record* reporter Bill Fritch. He penned a simple question in poetic form.

> *Oh, where are your bones*
> *Billy Boy, Billy Boy;*
> *Oh, where are your bones,*
> *Infamous Billy?*[286]

The poem, whether intended as humor, brought the real question to the surface. No one saw the Kid's bones in some years, and the petition served as affirmation they were there. The motion to intervene, in the eyes of the curious, was an attempt to keep those prying eyes from peeking.

The answer would have to wait. On December 6, 1961, the "Motion to Intervene" was filed by Humphrey and District Attorney Victor Breen on behalf of Louis Bowdre. The motion was a one-page document signed by Humphrey. It stated in part that the postal worker was related to Charlie Bowdre, who was buried in close proximity to the Kid. The bulk of his argument was dedicated to the disturbance of Bowdre's grave. Humphrey wrote that it was *"no longer possible to locate the site of either grave and that the granting of the relief prayed for in the Petition herein would result in disturbing the remains of his said deceased relative."*[287]

To bolster the motion, Assistant District Attorney Humphrey forwarded an exhibit. The final order of the De Baca County Court Case Number 2184, dated February 27, 1939, pitted the Maxwell and other local families against the late husband of the current defendant, John W. Allen. The families wanted the cemetery designated as public property, but a portion of the grounds was utilized by Allen for an irrigation ditch. He moved the barbed wire to accommodate this goal. Apparently, they feared he permanently altered the boundaries of the graveyard. De Baca County District Judge Harry L. Patton ruled that the cemetery was "vested in the general public" and Allen could not plow over the graves, remove or alter the fence, or change the boundaries of the site. The barbed wire fence was ordered back to its boundaries of January 1938.[288]

The 1939 exhibit document clarified some of Humphrey's arguments. The historical case reflected the shifting values and tensions between generations, but it also established ownership and responsibilities of the cemetery property. In effect, Humphrey believed the document established legal grounds for dismissal of the charges against Mrs. Allen. Additionally, the results of the 1939 case showed the historic importance of the cemetery in county records. Humphrey's move was a marked shift in defense tactics. It made Louis Bowdre's role as intervenor more central to his argument as well.[289]

Humphrey emphasized the disturbance of bodily remains at the Old Fort Sumner Cemetery. Unfortunately, there was little study of the family relationships that established standing for the strategy. In a genealogical glance at the intervenor, Louis A. Bowdre revealed no kinship link to Charlie Bowdre in six generations. Despite the fact they lived a state away and shared a surname, there appeared little or no close connection. Even then, Charlie Bowdre had living great-nephews and great-nieces across the country. Inversely, De Baca County and Humphrey openly questioned Telfer's claim of nearest kin to the outlaw. Unbeknownst to them, the argument posed a risk to Breen and Humphrey's defense if effectively used against them. It was doubtful they knew Louis Bowdre's kinship, but the key was whether anyone questioned the fact during the hearings.[290]

Louis Bowdre's past proved interesting. He was born on December 8, 1917 to George Washington and Joanna McAmis Bowdre of Meeker, Oklahoma. Although his family worked for the Katy & Cahill Railroad, several made state history. Cousin William H. Bowdre was a probate judge and Blaine County representative to the first Oklahoma state legislature in 1907.[291] Through an article on Judge Bowdre, much of Louis' own background is revealed. His forebears hailed from Ohio and through Kansas, not Georgia or Mississippi. Specifically, his parents were of Tennessee or Virginia roots.[292]

Regardless of the real connection to Charlie Bowdre, nationwide news coverage heralded the appearance of Louis Bowdre as intervenor in the case. This was echoed in the *Lincoln County News,* which faithfully reported the new wrinkle.

A third party in the case between Miss Lois Telfer and the De Baca county commissioners to remove Billy the Kid's body to his home grounds of Lincoln County has filed a motion to intervene in the court action.

Louis A. Bowdre of Bartlesville, Okla., who claims he is a relative of Charlie Bowdre, say he doesn't want any digging for Billy's bones going on as the grave might also contain the bones of Billy's buddy, Charlie Bowdre.

The Oklahoma [sic] Bowdre says that Charlie Bowdre is buried next to or very near William H. Bonney, and it's no longer possible to locate the site of either grave, and that excavation would result in disturbing the remains of his deceased relative.

Attorney C.C. Chase of Alamogordo, representing the Lincoln Countians who want to bring Billy home, and no dates for the hearing on the intervention have been set. A tentative date for hearing the actual motion to disinter Billy's remains had been set for December 15 but was postponed. The motion to intervene by the Oklahoma [sic] Bowdre must now be heard before the motion to disinter.[293]

The motion to intervene proved equally good and bad news for Chase. It gave him time to build a solid case, but an extra burden faced him in court. The motion made another appearance by Lois Telfer necessary in order to counter the intervenor's testimony. However, the death of Joe Sargent unnerved her, and the previous visits to Fort Sumner conjured bad memories. An unexpected visit to face angry constituents in De Baca County was not desired.

Telfer lingered in New York, but she continued her letters to contacts in New Mexico. Phil Cooke III, the publisher of the *Santa Fe New Mexican*, had intermittent contact with her by the beginning of December 1961. She praised his paper's coverage of the case. To further impress the publisher, Telfer flirted with an introduction to her friend Sylvester Vigilante and mentioned her association with author Mari Sandoz, the author of the novel *Old Jules*.[294]

I told Mr. S. Vigilante about your fine paper, and I am sure you will hear from him. Just returned from a reception at the New York Historical [Society], where I had a most pleasant visit with Mari Sandoz. She says to say "Hello." Next time I get to Santa Fe, I'll drop in to see you. "Vig" has spoken of you often.[295]

The large amount of press muddied the waters even more. Claims from "new relatives" appeared out of nowhere. Historian Bill Kelly received a letter from an "Iris Bowdre," who resided in Camden, New Jersey, in 1961. She claimed to be the closest surviving relative, and that Charlie's body was already removed by George Coe and reburied in their family cemetery. Of course, she was not the closest relative to Bowdre, nor was there any evidence of Coe's removal of a body. Iris Bowdre's claim reached *Real West* magazine. Upon reading this tale, Alan Rhodes fired off a letter of dispute. George Coe's daughter Elsa Perry was asked about this subject, but she denied Iris Bowdre's claim. Her father wanted all three bodies returned and re-buried at their ranch, but permission was needed from relatives before any movement could occur. George Coe gave up as he did not know where to find the families. In early December 1961, an Arizona woman named Mary Scott claimed to be a third cousin of Billy the Kid. She stated her mother was from the Bonney family, and stated "quite a few relatives" lived from her line. She favored De Baca County's view of the case, and further doubted the remains could be found. Mrs. Scott hinted about approaching the courts on the matter herself.[296]

Author Mari Sandoz knew Telfer in New York.
Author's Collection.

After the holidays, Judge Hensley set a new hearing date. The *Albuquerque Journal* published the announcement that a proceeding for the motion to intervene was scheduled for Wednesday, January 24, at 10 a.m. Louis Bowdre's personal appearance was not required, and Humphrey did not press for one at the time. Telfer decided not to appear as the decision was not on the fate of petition, but only on the intervenor.[297]

Telfer believed the opposition was obsessed with her direct family relationship with the Kid. In a January 17 letter to Phil Cooke, she rambled about the confusion between Bonney and McCarty surnames. She alluded that "Kathleen McCarthy" and her son Henry were different people altogether. Telfer used a historical notation, later identified as a typo, in Cooke's newspaper as her version of proof.

As Henry McCarty was about Billy's age, & his mother (Josie) short for Josephine, were no doubt friends. All lived in Silver City later. Mrs. Antrim's real name was <u>*Kathleen McCarthy*</u>*. Court clerks in those days were not noted for their spelling. Pat Garrett, who knew the Antrims well, said he Antrim always called her "Kathleen," & he was* <u>*right*</u>*.*

Vol. 1 #3 of your own "Territorian," Page 2, Col. 1, Bottom of Page: --Henry McCarty (note spelling) a petty thief was still in action in 1887, six years after Billy The Kid was dead! (1881)![298]

Lois Telfer hurt her own cause with the Cooke letter. She was defensive and wasted valuable time. In her letter, Telfer omitted any mention of the intervenor or her thoughts about the pending fortunes of the case. Most of all, the letter provided her opposition with ammunition against her. Seeds of doubt appeared in her claims of close family relationship to the Kid.

Meanwhile, Chase filed a "Response to Motion to Intervene" on January 11, 1962. In doing so, he contested the claim of Louis Bowdre based on his failure to establish grounds to intervene. Chase claimed Humphrey's motion was solely based on stopping Telfer's petition. Further, he countered that there was no intention of disturbing other remains. Humphrey appeared ready for this move, and he filed an answer in time for the hearing.[299]

On January 24, the hearing on intervenor rights reintroduced the courtroom drama. The proceedings lacked its prior headline-grabbing buzz, but the hearing lacked a final decision or a long list of witnesses. Yet, the importance of this side action became evident. If Louis Bowdre intervened, it was a partial victory to the De Baca County side. The only witness at the proceeding was 77-year-old John Tom "J.T." Perkins, the longtime resident of Fort Sumner who poured the concrete curbing at the Kid's supposed resting place decades earlier. During questioning on his actions in 1930, Perkins recalled two "old-timers" that disagreed on the exact location of the plot. They inspected the cemetery grounds, but they both insisted the plot was the proper location. The problem was both men stood 12 feet apart! After the two men spent considerable time in argument, they compromised. The exasperated Perkins poured the concrete once they decided on a location.[300]

Humphrey's revised "Answer to Petition" was filed on the day of the hearing. The document primarily admitted or denied various arguments in the petition, but included "facts" on Charlie Bowdre and the intervenor. While some of the information was reiteration of basic history facts, the greatest oversight of the entire case was within it. In the portion noting their first affirmative defense, Humphrey stated: *"That he [Louis] is next of kin of Charles Bowdre, deceased."*[301] Although news reports pronounced this, it seems strange that an intelligent and detail-oriented lawyer as Humphrey made this key mistake on a legal document. The Assistant District Attorney either assumed Louis Bowdre was next of kin without vetting him, or he was misled. Either way, Humphrey was lucky. News coverage focused on Telfer and largely ignored Louis

Bowdre's lineage. Charlie's surviving nieces and nephews slipped off unnoticed in their stories.[302]

Fort Sumner contractor J.T. Perkins.
Courtesy of Mrs. Marsha Perkins.

At the hearing, the issue of Louis Bowdre's standing as next of kin never reached Judge Hensley's ears. In his ruling, his decision was driven by the lack of a definite burial location. If Telfer and the Lincoln County contingent won their case, and removal ensued, there was a good chance the remains of Charlie Bowdre or Thomas O'Folliard could be disturbed. If buried in the same plot or next to each other, the 12-foot difference between the two countering opinions of the Kid's burial spot ensured enough room for a mistake. Given these circumstances, Judge Hensley permitted Louis Bowdre the right to intervene. The order was filed on January 29, 1962, and the hearing date was set for March 12. Tired of the hyperbole associated with the case, Judge Hensley stated that the "court is not inclined to view with other petitions to intervene."[303]

The identification of the Kid's grave location was a difficult, but not impossible, task. Clarissa Fuller, reporting for the *Albuquerque Tribune*, hinted at the possibility while simultaneously noting the futility of the effort. In the January 27th issue, her interviews of Fort Sumner residents revealed that the Kid's burial apparel gave a narrow window of hope for identification. The three large brass safety pins used to affix Pete Maxwell's large black coat might still exist. Vicente Otero, who prepared the body for burial, noted that the brass pins constituted proof of the correct individual.[304]

In hindsight, the opportunity for Lincoln County was all but lost at that moment. Only a sliver of hope remained for Telfer and Chase after Judge Hensley ruled in favor of the intervenor. The battle for the body of Billy the Kid was nearly a year old. Whether intentional or not, Humphrey outmaneuvered Chase with his witness. Bowdre's standing was equal to Lois Telfer once Judge Hensley ruled. The uphill climb to bring the body of Billy the Kid to Lincoln got steeper.

CHAPTER SEVEN

DECREE

By February 1, 1962, the application of Lois Telfer to transfer the body of Billy the Kid was a over a month from a showdown with De Baca County officials and Louis Bowdre, the Bartlesville, Oklahoma postal worker who successfully filed to intervene. The advantage was clearly on De Baca County's side. Bowdre was ready and able to travel to court, while Telfer waffled in New York. C.C. Chase, without either Telfer or the late Joe Sargent, was fighting a campaign largely on his own. He needed Telfer's presence as a witness in March.

Meanwhile, news coverage kept a measured pace and the legal maneuvering continued behind the scenes. Chester Chope of the *El Paso Herald-Post* penned an update in his February 5 column of "This Fabulous Southwest."

If Billy the Kid's body is moved after all these years from Fort Sumner to Lincoln County, it looks as if his pals—Tom O'Folliard and Charles Bowdre—may have to go with him," the Carlsbad Current Argus observed editorially, "Billy, Tom and Charlie are buried in the same plot....J.T. Perkins of Fort Sumner, who built a curbstone around the plot in 1930, said he didn't know which grave was which. He and two other men engaged in a bit of guesswork in laying out the curbstone...If Mrs. Lois Telfer of New York (who claims to be the outlaw's only known relative) is successful in her efforts (to get Billy's remains removed) it might be best to move all three graves. This would insure that Billy's bones were among those removed.[305]

The speculation only increased with such stories. There seemed no end to possibilities posed by reporters and local residents. Some suggested the Kid's body might not be in Fort Sumner at all. That kind of doubt could be used in court by Assistant District Attorney John Humphrey, and he knew where to look. William V. Morrison of El Paso was welcomed as an "insider" to the "Friends of Billy the Kid," but he had his own agenda. Largely ignored by the group, Morrison was open to anyone that would listen. A cousin in Fort Sumner tipped off Humphrey to Morrison's research.[306]

On January 30, Humphrey wrote Morrison on his official letterhead. He asked about his research, particularly the relationship of Lois Telfer to the Kid. Humphrey stated in part, *"Naturally I am very interested in learning what the results of your search were, if any. I am enclosing a copy of the genealogy which she has submitted to us...The case has been set for trial on March 12, 1962. Do you think it might be possible for you to be here on that date? We could pay at least a part of your expenses."*[307]

On February 8, Morrison responded to Humphrey with a three-page letter that provided plenty of ammunition for the De Baca County side. *"In my opinion,"* Morrison wrote, *"the chart is not complete. I fail to find any mention of the Kid's half-brother [sic], brother or cousin, whichever the other child proves to be. There is a doubt that the mother entered Colorado and New Mexico with two children. The marriage to Wm. H. Antrim recorded in the legal records in Santa Fe is sufficient proof as the two boys were there then."*[308] He believed *"that, at this late date, it would almost be impossible for Lois Telfer to establish her heirship in this case."*[309] Morrison asked if Humphrey had filed a motion for her attorney to produce wills and documents that further proved her relationship, and a comment that he advised Chase that the Telfer petition lacked witnesses relating to the ownership of the cemetery. He forwarded Humphrey copies of his research.[310]

The damage to Telfer's petition became evident. Morrison probably never believed he betrayed her cause. After all, their aims varied from his goals. The irony was that neither met them, and the only beneficiary of the exchange was letter was Humphrey. By his advice to Humphrey, valuable support was lost in Lincoln County. In addition to Morrison, Humphrey corresponded with Mullin. He had insider's knowledge of Telfer's personal correspondence. Unlike Morrison, the historian kept clear of active involvement in the case. On February 6, Mullin wrote Humphrey, and he received a response eight days later. From the response, it appeared the detail-oriented historian was seeking, not giving, information on Bonney surname. He was trying to satisfy his own curiosity about Telfer's lineage.[311]

Although the chance for the petition's success was slim, there were small victories. On February 13, Judge Hensley signed an order to block the dismissal of the petition prior to the March 12 hearing. By throwing out the motion to dismiss, it meant time for personal appearances by interested parties. In fact, it was fully expected that Lois Telfer would attend the March hearing. Sylvester Vigilante wrote on his interesting letterhead—that of a hanged cowboy from a tree limb—to *New Mexico Territorian* publisher Philip Cooke on February 17th. He announced to Cooke that Lois Telfer was bound for Fort Sumner in early March for the hearing. Vigilante admitted that her attendance was necessary as *"Lois is the only living relative (?). "*[312]

Meanwhile, the newspapers trumpeted the March 12 "showdown" for weeks. Columnist George Dixon, writing for the "Washington Scene" that ran in numerous newspapers, dedicated an entire story on February 2. He queried Charles Fischer, the publisher of the *Clovis News-Journal*, who claimed the entire issue began as a publicity stunt that "got out of hand."[313] Reporter Dudley M. Lynch, writing for the *Alamogordo Daily News*, summarized the hype on February 21 by noting the "showdown" promised a packed courthouse and foreshadowed "a legislatic [sic] shoot-'em up."[314]

At the beginning of March 1962, the "showdown" loomed and expectations fell short. The news vacuum that extended over a month, the publicity was largely repetitive. There was every reason to expect Lois Telfer in Fort Sumner, although she shied away. The *El Paso Herald-Post* reported, *"Lois Telfer, a New York City beautician, says she is the nearest kin to Billy. She is expected to so testimy [sic] when she appears in court."*[315] The Lincoln County Board of Commissioners, at their March 5th meeting, decided to inform Chase that no funding was available for interment in Lincoln as the body was needed within bounds before any approval could be considered. On March 6, Humphrey submitted an additional witness list for the forthcoming hearing. Testimony was requested from Carlos Clancy, L.F. Silva, mortician Walter Julien, J.T. Perkins, and Walter Wright.[316]

More personal drama entered the fray. Judge Hensley's 88-year-old mother, Sophronia Ellen Hensley, died on March 7 in nearby Clovis, New Mexico. Only five days before the trial, her eldest son was saddled with one of most publicized cases in the state. His elderly father survived her, but the personal weight of arranging services combined with the building barrage of press interest must have taken a personal toll on Judge Hensley. The service for his mother was Friday, March 9, at 3 p.m., and the hearing was reset for Tuesday, March 13, at 9:00 a.m. Humphrey wrote Morrison after the trial that the Judge was under *"considerable strain from mothers [sic] death."*[317]

On Tuesday morning, a large crowd gathered around the De Baca County Courthouse in Fort Sumner. Reporter John McMillion described it as an overcrowded "musty old courtroom" that relegated most onlookers to the hallway. The cluster of reporters contended for room alongside the interested citizens. Although a crowded courthouse, there was a most interesting feature inside. In the courtroom hall, there was a giant mural of Billy the Kid and a number of his associates completed by artist Russell Vernon Hunter in 1935.[318]

The death of Judge Hensley's mother appeared to have one effect. He was in no mood to draw out any hearing about moving the body. The entire hearing lasted an hour and a half, but the crushing crowd may have factored in its brevity. Humphrey was taken aback, as he admitted afterward. Newspaper reporters called the hearing "anti-climactic," although both sides of the debate hardly felt that way. Judge Hensley stuck to the basic particulars the hearing required and nothing more. In his mind, he had a job to do.[319]

A partial reason for the anticlimactic atmosphere involved the lack of witnesses from Lincoln County. After much speculation about her appearance, Lois Telfer was nowhere to be seen. Of course, she was represented by C.C. Chase. Later, she wrote Mullin that a great fire destroyed the salon she worked in, causing great hardship and not allowing her to fly west for the hearing. However, no other representative from Lincoln County testified at the hearing. Chase fended for himself, with only his knowledge and skill to face bad fortune and press. Their once-fevered cause was graded down by a year of tragedy and ill-feeling.[320]

In the end, only one witness testified: Louis A. Bowdre. His daughter Sue accompanied him, and years later remembered the long drive to Fort Sumner. Along the way, he adamantly told his daughter that this was his duty. There was no doubt that the postman believed in his cause. In the hearing coverage, newspaper reporters repeated the incorrect claim that Louis was *"Charlie Bowdre's last kin."*[321] The *Lubbock Avalanche-Journal* published his version of the mistaken family relationship. *"Bowdre, who said Charlie was the son of Frank Bowdre, a brother of Louis Bowdre's grandfather, George W. Sr., objected to any attempt to move the Kid's bones because he said it might disturb the bones of his relative."*[322]

The problem lay in the question of relation. Charlie was a son of Albert Rees, not Frank Bowdre. It was irrelevant whether this was simply an oversight, but the error cast doubt on the entire relationship. This could have been established in the legal research prior to the hearing, and should have been. Scant resources for genealogical research existed at the time of the hearing, placing more reliance on family information.[323]

Judge Hensley opened the hearing with an admission. He found little precedent with the case, but viewed similar cases that involved family decisions in moving burial locations. A recounting of oft-spoken facts on the Kid's demise was followed by witness testimony. With no Lois Telfer available to counter his testimony, Louis Bowdre's testimony carried incredible weight. Furthermore, he was brief and on point. Bowdre repeated his reason for Fort Sumner to retain the body. On cross, Chase asked Bowdre why he had never visited Charlie's grave before. In doing so, he pointed a possible lack of interest. However, this proved a bad tactic. *"We had sufficient interest,"* Bowdre shot back. *"but insufficient funds."*[324]

For all his ability, Chase was outmaneuvered and out of legal ammunition. By choosing to pin down Louis Bowdre's lack of interest in the cemetery, and build on Telfer's claim of gravesite neglect, hopes of an effective strategy faltered. There was no way to counter Bowdre's testimony without the perception of bullying a hard-working, cash-strapped family man. The public read that Telfer failed to appear, taking Chase's hope with her. The petition was at the mercy of the court.

Judge Hensley wasted little time with his ruling. He declared that *"in the last days of his [the Kid's] life, it became apparent that Lincoln County was the place where he least desired to live and die."*[325] He used the escape from Lincoln and the deaths associated with it as an example. Most importantly, Ms. Telfer or Mrs. Allen did not know the exact location of the grave. Time combined with the floods and other natural means, made location impossible without the reality of disturbing other remains. Although Judge Hensley gave each side 10 days to file objections, he ruled the motion to move the body was denied. Billy the Kid's body would remain in Fort Sumner.[326]

The hearing ended quickly, but with a false sense of historical finality. The reporters hurriedly scribbled notes. The *Lubbock Avalanche-Journal* featured a front-page snap of a victorious Louis Bowdre in front of Hunter's mural. He stood straight between the images of Billy the Kid and Charlie Bowdre. There was a picture of the victorious De Baca contingent at the memorial as well.[327]

Humphrey hurriedly wrote Morrison to return his papers the following day. Apparently, he was present in Fort Sumner, but lost in the crowds at the courthouse. Humphrey wrote Morrison that he never thought Judge Hensley would grant Lois Telfer's petition. The Assistant District Attorney admitted he did not want an abbreviated hearing. *"He [Judge Hensley] wanted to cut the trial short and practically forced us to stipulate that the Petitioner, Miss Telfer, was the next of kin, as trying this issue would have taken quite a bit of time."*[328]

Morrison shot back a typed letter the following day. This response was far more critical of Telfer than his previous communication. It is likely Morrison believed the entire court process fell short of reality. In any case, he left Fort Sumner immediately after the hearing for an appointment.

I wanted to visit after the trial, but I had a tentative appointment in Lubbock that afternoon and it was snowing when I left Fort Sumner. I would have stayed over if Miss Telfer had shown for examination on her heirship. I was never convinced that she could prove it sufficiently to stay in Court and I did not think that she would ever appear in Court.[329]

Morrison complimented Judge Hensley for the "broad and sincere manner" in handling the case findings. He viewed the Judge's decision as decisive, and the "stipulations" placed on kinship matters prevented future petitions of this kind. He believed their relationship to the deceased was "not the real issues before the Court."[330]

As Chase introduced his photos to show intent and extent of commercialization of the Kid's grave in that area, it recalled memories of the numerous photos I made in 1949 of the commercialization made of Kid in Lincoln County, New Mexico.

Had you contacted me earlier in the case or I had reason to believe it would go trial, I would have prevailed upon my cousin in Roswell to file an intervenor motion where we could have defrayed the costs of depositions in taking Miss Telfer's testimony on the issue of nearest of kin, which would have removed her from the picture. I advertised widely in 1949 without avail. However, the end result was attained for all practical purposes. Diligent researchers will never believe the Kid's family name was Bonney.[331]

The two letters between Humphrey and Morrison settled certain questions. Morrison's claim of photographs which countered Fort Sumner's commercial intent, and his willingness to share those, proved he was a skeptic, and later an opponent, to Telfer's cause. However, this could have been all talk. Humphrey himself never realized that his own intervenor's relationship as "next of kin" could have been exposed. He was extremely lucky.

The Lincoln County representatives endured their bad fortune, and their newspaper stories reflected the bitterness. However, space was limited and the tone was like a mournful obituary. *The Lincoln County News* stated "Billy's bones rest in peace" next to local news about paving county roads. Perhaps as a last jab, the first line read, *"The dust and weeds covering Billy the Kid's grave in DeBaca County will not be disturbed."*[332] It was also a last salute to the late Joe Sargent, whose efforts were credited as *"a friend of Miss Telfer during her several visits to Lincoln County."*[333]

The actions following the hearing deepened the bitterness. Newspapers trumpeted the headlines around the country. The opponents of the Telfer petition took a victory lap by publishing the group picture at the "Pals" monument. Flanked on side by mortician Julian, Robert Colter, De Baca County Commissioner Bill Franks, and District Attorney Breen, and on the other by Louis Bowdre, Humphrey, and Frank Silva, the image was tasteful and solemn. The participants captured a moment in history, and the Associated Press snapshot was published in C.C. Chase's hometown paper, the *Alamogordo Daily News.*[334]

In a way, historians dismissed the whole matter when it disappeared outside the region. Historian Jeff Dykes, who then lived in Washington, D.C., was informed by a postcard of the outlaw mailed from Roswell. A friend briefly wrote on the reverse, *"I hear the New Mexico Courts have decided to let the bones of this character stay in Fort Sumner.*"[335] Other historians shrugged off the matter as a publicity stunt. After all, the entire matter was about publicity in the first place. It revolved around unproven descendants and a fistfight between jurisdictions for a famous corpse. No one dismantled billboards or closed museums over Judge Hensley's decision.[336]

Despite the publicity, Humphrey filed notice for the signing of Judge Hensley's decree on March 30, 1962. After the initial sting of news reports passed, he arranged to meet the Jurist in Clovis, where he regularly sat in court. Judge Hensley, with both Chase and Humphrey, signed the official paperwork on April 6. De Baca County Clerk Judy Marshall promptly filed the decree on April 9, and officially ended Case 3255, Lois Telfer's claim for the body of Billy the Kid.[337]

DECREE

This matter coming on for hearing in open Court at Fort Sumner, New Mexico, this 13th day of March, 1962, petitioner appearing by her attorney, C.C. Chase, Jr., respondents, Board of County Commissioners appearing in person and by Victor C. Breen, District Attorney of the Tenth Judicial District and John Humphrey, Jr., Assistant District Attorney, and respondent Mrs. J.W. Allen appearing in person and by her attorneys Victor C. Breen and John Humphrey, Jr., and the intervenor, Louis A. Bowdre, appearing in person and by his attorneys, Victor C. Breen and John Humphrey, Jr., and the Court having heard the evidence presented and being fully advised in the premises,

FINDS:

1. That Charles Bowdre was killed at Fort Sumner, New Mexico, in the in the year 1880.

2. That said Charles Bowdre was thereafter buried in the Fort Sumner Cemetery, where his remains now are.

3. That William H. Bonney, alias Billy the Kid, was killed at Fort Sumner, New Mexico, on July 14, 1881.

4. That said William H. Bonney was thereafter buried in the Fort Sumner Cemetery, beside or very near the grave of the said Charles Bowdre, and that the remains of the said William H. Bonney are still buried in the said Fort Sumner Cemetery.

5. That due to the lapse of time and natural causes, it is no longer possible to locate the site of the graves of the said William H. Bonney, deceased, and said Charles Bowdre, deceased.

6. That over the years, large numbers of persons have been buried in the said Fort Sumner Cemetery and that the said Cemetery as it now exists is very thickly planted with graves.

7. That a search for the grave of the said William H. Bonney, deceased, in order to disinter said body, will inevitably lead to disturbing the remains of other persons, buried in said cemetery, including the said Charles Bowdre, deceased.

8. That petitioner Lois Telfer is the next of kin of said William H. Bonney, deceased.

9. That intervenor, Louis A. Bowdre, is next of kin of said Charles Bowdre, deceased.

WHEREFORE, the Court makes the following

CONCLUSIONS OF LAW

1.   That the court has jurisdiction of the subject matter and of the parties hereto.

2.   That the relief prayed for in the Petition herein cannot be granted since the site of the grave of William H. Bonney, deceased, cannot be located.

3.   That the relief prayed for in the Petition herein cannot be granted since a search for the grave of William H. Bonney, deceased, in order to disinter said body, will inevitably lead to disturbing the remains of other persons, buried in said cemetery, including the said Charles Bowdre, deceased.

WHEREFORE IT IS ORDERED, ADJUDGED AND DECREED

that the Petition of Lois Telfer be, and the same hereby is, dismissed and that the petitioner take nothing and that the action be, and it hereby is, dismissed on the merits.[338]

The decree served as the final word in some ways, and left others wide open. It was the end of the official effort to bring the body of Billy the Kid back to Lincoln. The most obvious problem with the document was the erroneous "next of kin" findings, which if known would have forced the issue further. However, the case was lost by the time the decree was issued. Only ten days were required, yet Judge Hensley waited even longer and no objection was lodged.

Oddly, public reaction ramped up in some quarters of the region after the decree was known. In Las Vegas, New Mexico, the publisher of the local newspaper, L.R. Finch, along with Denver author Milton W. Callon, challenged De Baca County residents to prove the Kid was actually in the cemetery. Announced from the *Lincoln County News,* the reaction was based on an old article in Finch's paper, the *Las Vegas Optic,* which stated that a "fearless skelelogist" dug up the body not long after his burial. The article referenced an unknown person who intended to keep the bones of the outlaw together—for display purposes. It stated, *"Let's dig him up. Let's see who it is. Let's not be defrauding the public. If it can be proven that his bones are where they attest to be, then you have a legitimate claim. Are you afraid of our historical challenge?"*[339]

Meanwhile, Lois Telfer was cloistered in New York City, far from the impact of the petition hearing. Mullin wrote her, but it was not until May 22 that she responded. The tone seemed one of resentment mixed with resignation. She began by explaining her absence from the hearing.

As you know, I was unable to make the trip to N.M. this year. Was a victim of a Big 10 alarm fire at work. The big supermarket next to   the cosmetic salon burned out. Our place completely gone, mostly heavy black smoke. I got out all right, after falling on top of a cop, who was trying to help me.[340]

Telfer was pragmatic after the loss in court, and saw value in the added attention and care for the grave. Still, she was angry at her opponents in De Baca County.

Billy shall Rest in Peace although I hear the Judge in Fort Sumner got some "hot" letters from important people in my favor. If all this gets those bastard politicians in De Baca County to clean up the grave & its surroundings, I feel my efforts are not in vain.[341]

Although Lois Telfer wrote of pyrrhic victories, the effects of Judge Hensley's decree reverberated through the lives of the participants and shaped opinion for decades. For De Baca County residents, there was little fear of a repeated petition by other relatives. Assistant District Attorney John Humphrey, Jr. achieved what he set out to do. Through passion and pure luck, Humphrey won. Incidentally, Lois Telfer was not the only "next of kin." Her brother Richard lived in Michigan. If the decree was incorrect on one side, it was equally erroneous on the other. For those opposing forces, time was kind to none.

CHAPTER EIGHT

HISTORICAL WARS

In April 1962, the petition of Lois Telfer to reinter the body of Billy the Kid was official denied by Judge Elias T. Hensley. While the official hearing ended, the argument festered much longer. Telfer's remained in touch with New Mexico friends for several years longer, but the associated historians and surrogates kept the matter in the court of public opinion. Had most of the major participants from the hearing survived into the 2000s, there might have been longevity. Instead, most of them passed away within a decade of the proceeding and replaced most of the argument with silence. The year-long battle between representatives of two counties for famous bones changed hearts and minds in how historians look at Old West history. Its importance in the lexicon of the famous outlaw should not be overlooked.

The historians and researchers gave voice to the matter once the case ended. The loudest voices belonged to Morrison and Phil Rasch, the latter absent from the scene while the hearing occurred. Rasch's ability often irritated people. His articles picked on Lois Telfer for some time after the hearing. One of them, "Old Problems, New Answers," published in the *New Mexico Historical Review* in January 1965, busted open a whole new feud between Telfer and her supporters against Rasch and William J. Carson of Burbank, California. He mailed several letters to Telfer, who ignored them. She did not know Carson or his research relationship with Phil Rasch.[342]

"Old Problems, New Answers" appeared nearly three years after the hearing, but the corresponding reaction proved wounds never healed. Rasch's article took direct aim at Lois Telfer's relationship with the Kid, starting with his presentation of facts and documentation. However, in the third paragraph he got personal in his comments.

There was little difficulty in demonstrating that Henry McCarty and William Bonney were one and the same individual, and the discrepancy in the names of his mother was apparently satisfactorily resolved by Miss Lois Telfer, assertedly a collateral descendant of the Bonney family, stated her family's tradition recounted that the Bonney marriage had proved an unhappy one and that the wife had resumed her maiden name following the death of her husband. She was, she said, planning to write a book about her notorious kinsman and for that reason could not make any data from the family records available to other researchers. To date her book has not appeared and no substantiating evidence has been forthcoming, which has raised serious doubts of whether the latter exists.[343]

Rasch credited a study undertaken by Carson. The latter compared document sources in New York, and he concluded that Henry McCarty had different parents. Lois Telfer slapped down Rasch in a letter to Mullin on September 5, 1965.

How do you like this enclosed piece of junk? When I was out in New Mexico I asked 4 people, who had "seen" Rasch. Their comments, as follows:

#1	*"A real Jerk"*
#2	*"A nuisance"*
#3	*"A Pest"*
#4	*"Forget Him"*

No one in authority ever heard of "Carson." After my not answering 3 Letters, he wrote a real nasty letter to L.C. [Lincoln County] News. Guess these 2 guys just like to get mail.[344]

Telfer's rebuke might have ended the conversation, but Carson exacerbated the issue with a column focused on a debate about the Kid's birth information. Although he made no direct reference to Telfer, Carson intimated that "William H. Bonney" was probably not authentic on the existing documentation. It was the words in his final paragraph which drew Telfer's ire. *"My goodness, if a Bonney can be proven in this story I will be the first to hail it. I think this nonsense has gone far enough. What the hell, I don't want to be related to 'Billy the Kid.'"*[345]

Alan Rhodes was equally incensed by Carson's column, and he retaliated with one of his own. The son of novelist Eugene Manlove Rhodes defended Telfer with vigor. He wrote, *"Mr. Carson's letter was full of gross mistakes, as any serious researchers of Billy the Kid will admit. So I am writing this article so your readers of the Lincoln County News will not be misinformed and disillusioned."*[346] Rhodes related there was proof about Telfer's upstate connections, and that the Kid's family lived at several addresses in New York City. He boosted Telfer's relationship as a "third cousin of Billy the Kid," and his father's connection to George Coe. They *"were good friends, fought with Billy the Kid all thru [sic] the Lincoln County War, and there was never any doubt in his mind that Billy the Kid's real name was William H. Bonney."*[347]

In the later portion of his letter to the editor, Alan Rhodes unleashed his vitriol at Carson. He questioned the credibility of the researcher.

Doesn't it seem strange to you, dear reader, that a man who has been known known for 100 years as William H. Bonney should in the last decade or two, have doubts cast upon the truth of his name being William H. Bonney, with some people claiming his name was Antrim, others claiming it was McCarty? To me it is asinine.[348]

Rhodes concluded by warning readers not to be misled by Carson's letter. "Truth is stronger than fiction," he wrote before thanking the editor and planning a visit later a few months later for the annual tour to his father's grave. It was a strong and compelling counterpunch to Carson and Rasch, but it also fired up William Morrison.[349]

Never shrinking from a fight, Morrison sent in a four-column letter on March 6, 1966. Rhodes' comment about revised history, along with his own theories about the Kid, sent the legal professional into a tailspin. He asked the editor if Rhodes had legal citations available for his use, *"or if Mr. Rhodes just wants to carry on the fued [sic]."[350]* Morrison inserted himself into the argument, and continued his piece on the opposition to his past attempts. If he followed a single, well-crafted argument, and not a historical lecture on "Brushy Bill" Roberts, Morrison may have fared better in print. Instead, he delved into the diverse topics and legal arguments before finally addressing Alan Rhodes.[351]

Mr. Rhodes like Mr. Will Keleher failed to find criminal case file in the United States District Court wherein Kid pled to indictment returned by grand jury murder, thusly: Now comes the Plaintiffs herein by their District Attorney, S.M. Barnes, Esq., and the defendant Henry Antrim, Alias "Kid" in his proper Person...and the grand jurors knew the Kid as Henry Antrim in the 1880's.

To get the meat of the allegations made by Miss Telfer in her Petition filed in De Baca County District Court, wherein she filed copies of her

Bonney family tree, one of which was furnished the undersigned by the Distrcit [sic] Attorney prior to trial of said cause, and I am checking this now. I fail to find where her relative, William Bonney, married Miss McCarty; there is no mention Kid's brother, Joseph Antrim or his step-father, in this family tree, and no connection of Henry Antrim, alias Kid, to her Bonney family.[352]

The detailed letter presented a number of legal points. However, the message dispersed these throughout the communication. The reader might have missed them.

Furthermore, Miss Lois Telfer, Plaintiff, failed to show for trial of the case to present testimony or evidence of her relationship to Kid. I heard the Court deliver his opinion in a very broad and sincere manner. He left no room for doubt. Judge Henlsey [sic] dismissed her action and it stands dismissed. Probably Mr. Rhodes is relying upon Miss Telfer's family history in hopes of proving Billy's grandfather and uncle owned property in New York State in the 1820's.

It is hoped that Miss Telfer informs Mr. Rhodes she failed to appear in her own behalf and that her case was dismissed when he visits her this summer.[353]

The feud survived William Morrison's March 1966 article. After all, the central argument was between Carson (and Rasch) and Rhodes. Carson waded back into the fight with another letter in late May, and it was published in the June 2nd *Lincoln County News*. In another long piece, he detailed his research findings while slamming both Rhodes and Telfer. Carson delved in and wrote, *"I have been working with Mr. Philip Rasch, another writer and researcher for about three years now on the specific subject of the genealogy of Billy the Kid. In the past couple of years several interesting facts have come to light."*[354]

Carson mixed positive and negative messages. Respectfully, he referenced Morrison's co-authored book with Leland Sonnichsen, *Alias Billy the Kid* and a new book by Waldo E. Koop, *Billy the Kid: the Trail of a Kansas Legend*. However, his barbs against Lois Telfer continued.

We wrote to Miss Telfer to try and find out what she knew, but for one reason or another she never answered us. Silence is golden, it was concluded that her claims must stand as a tenable hypthesis until they were disproved. This seems to have been accomplished by Morrison in his article to you April 7. It was very interesting to note that Miss Telfer had brought her claim to relationship with Billy the Kid to court and the case was dismissed due to lack of evidence. Until I read this article I did not know that the case had gone that far. All I was aware of was the results of extensive research.[355]

William Carson was partially incorrect with this statement. Telfer ignored their letters, but that hardly meant she admitted defeat or that the court decision disproved a claim of relationship due to lack of evidence. Judge Hensley dismissed the case due to the lack of an exact grave location, and the impact of disturbing other remains. The decree acknowledged Telfer's relationship. Also, Morrison's article presented research possibilities, and brought valid questions, but did not disprove Telfer's relationship to the Kid.

Mr. Alan Rhodes, in reply to my article of February 10, 1966, wanted to know why, after 100 years of being accepted, the name Bonney should now be questioned?

In all due respect to him, I could say the information included in the article should have been self explainatory! [sic] I suppose the reason for so much present interest in the Bonney name comes from the various claims people have made concerning it. Some claimed to have been the

Kid himself, while others merely distant relatives of our dashing pigeon for the Lincoln County War. Also, the element of time, and researchers interested in this subject, have produced a combination which brough [sic] new evidence to light. Material on this subject has been hard to find and even harder to authenticate.

This brings Miss Telfer to mnd [sic] once again. If she seriously believes she is related to Billy the Kid, she has been up against the same problems of collecting evidence as men in this field who are professionals and can't find anything! Evidence acceptable in a court of law, which would be conclusive on the subject, would be next to impossible to find. It is a small wonder that she lost the case mentioned by Mr. Morrison in your paper, and is reluctant to answer letters questioning her on the subject, which I mentioned! If she can prove her case more power to her. We just cannot find anything to do her murh [sic] good.[356]

The back-and-forth "letter to the editor" war trailed off. Some 11 years later, Morrison wrote an interested researcher that rumors indicated *"the Kid's name was Henry McCarty but no documentation."*[357] When warring with Alan Rhodes, he stopped short of fulling endorsing the McCarty name to disprove Telfer's relationship. Carson was correct on one point. Discovery of new material proved next to impossible on the subject. As time went on, Carson and Morrison felt isolated.

If Carson and Morrison experienced futility, publisher Paul Baker was long out of a job by this time. He personally endorsed Telfer and the Lincoln County group, and by using the *Lincoln County News* as the "mouthpiece" of the movement, Baker had the most to lose. In June 1961, the newspaper sold to a partnership of Paul Payton and W.J. Olds. Despite his writing role, he quietly departed the area. In 1966, Carson and Morrison were writing to owner Payton, not Baker.[358] .

Telfer's opponents suffered their own misfortunes. Although credited for their restoration program in Lincoln, John and Nan Boylan were frustrated with the Old Lincoln County Memorial Commission. In November 1964, John Boylan formally resigned and the couple went abroad for a time. Nan Boylan was given a year's leave at half her salary, but Secretary-Treasurer Pfingsten rejected the arrangement after he discovered the state never approved the deal. Edward Penfield took over as curator during their absence. In turn, he hired a new assistant at $200 per month named Nora Henn. While members and officials frequently changed during this period, these changes eroded the influence of the Boylans.[359]

After the Boylans returned from their European trip in June 1965, control of the Old Lincoln County Memorial Commission changed. Chairwoman Fran Sawyer convinced Penfield to retain Nan Boylan as another assistant. After rejecting the salary arrangement, Pfingsten departed from his role as secretary-treasurer. He was replaced by Carrizozo businessman Johnson Stearns, who approved Chairwoman Sawyer's request. The subject proved rancorous as tourism in Lincoln declined. In August, Nan Boylan accepted a job offer in Santa Fe and resigned.[360]

Nan Boylan still wielded influence as she exited the leadership. About the time she resigned, Nan Boylan and Commissioner Sawyer ousted Penfield as curator. Paul Gardner, a professional living in Italy, was selected to replace him. However, more problems surfaced when Gardner delayed his move from Europe to fulfill obligations. Penfield stayed in a temporary capacity, but he found a new position in December. Mrs. Boylan and Colonel Lusk found a temporary replacement as curator, but their prospect withdrew. She then opposed the new bookkeeper, Mrs. Henn. Penfield complained that good businesspeople were difficult to find. Subsequently, her artist husband Walter fell ill. The drama prompted a letter from Johnson Stearns to Gardner for his speedy arrival.[361]

For Lincoln, change was inevitable. The internal strife within the Old Lincoln County Memorial Commission was temporary. Nora Henn rose from bookkeeper to prominent historian, and the Boylans moved to Santa Fe. The Commission's first generation gave way to another with a different focus. New historians and methodologies came on the scene. Eve Ball, a former schoolteacher, emerged as a primary historian during this period. Her book on local resident Lily Klasner, entitled *My Girlhood Among Outlaws*, offered a new perspective of Billy the Kid and his various friendships. About the same time, Mullin released his edited work on Maurice Fulton's history of the Lincoln County War.[362]

The "Friends of Billy the Kid" faded into obscurity as many core members died over the course of the next decade. From 1966 to 1970, five key supporters of Lois Telfer passed away. Paul Blazer, 75, passed away in Tularosa in February 1966. Her great friend, Helena Coe LaMay, 67, died of cancer in May 1968. The new decade saw far more devastating losses. The legal face of the group, attorney C.C. Chase, remained in practice. He carried the burden of two historical losses: the legal loss to bring back Billy the Kid and an attempt to rehabilitate the reputation of his grandfather, Albert Fall, of the infamous Teapot Dome scandal. By decade's end, his health was undermined. He died on January 7, 1970 at only 46 years of age. Telfer's good friend, Sylvester Vigilante, was nearly 80 when he died that August. Although a decade younger than "Vig," Alan Hinman Rhodes passed away in November 1970.[363]

Early deaths also struck the opponents and other contemporaries of Lois Telfer's case as hard as those of her supporters. In 1966, the Honorable Elias T. Hensley was promoted to a new position as chief judge of the New Mexico Board of Appeals. He moved to Santa Fe, but after only a year, he died suddenly on November 22, 1967. Tragedy befell District Attorney Victor Breen on December 1, 1971, when he was shot and killed outside his home in Tucumcari, New Mexico. He was headed for court on the second day of a murder trial of a 17-year-old boy when an assailant fired a round from a high-powered rifle. Victor C. Breen, 55, was the country's third district attorney to be killed in the line of duty.[364]

With so many deaths within a decade of the case, there were few supporters who kept in touch with Lois Telfer. The New York beautician vanished from view. She never wrote the book Rasch expected. In the eyes of historians, Telfer became a footnote to Brushy Bill Roberts, and her claims were largely either cast aside or parsed. Once time passed and passions cooled after Judge Hensley's ruling, the assumptions made by the court or newspapers deserved further investigation. Yet there was little desire to do so.[365]

By 1976, Lois Telfer's case was largely forgotten, but the grave and adjoining land occasionally received press attention. The stone headstone marker contributed by Coloradan James Warner in 1940 was pilfered in 1950, during the height of the "Brushy Bill" appearance. It was finally identified 26 years later, when Granbury, Texas farmer Gaylon Wright realized the fancy stone on his property was the stolen marker. Only when a couple from Granbury visited Fort Sumner and noticed the missing stone and its appearance, they realized Wright's icon was indeed the Warner marker. Despite its brevity as a burial marker, Fort Sumner applauded its return.[366] Plans for a park and new museum on the property were long-range plans. In March 1967, officials purchased Mrs. Allen's 130 acres of land through a bond issue. An additional 50 acres of the old military grounds was transferred to the existing museum. The catalyst for the latter was local residents Joe and Marilyn Bowlin, who revitalized the exhibit into the Old Fort Museum six years later. The consolidation of park and museum was a positive step. On June 30, 1973, Fort Sumner Park was officially dedicated.[367]

In Lincoln, preservation plans changed over time. However, the old turf battles raged. Funding shortages haunted the Old Lincoln County Memorial Commission in acquisitions and upgrades, and this was not lost on the artists, led by John Meigs and Peter Hurd. A renaissance of western art and architecture surged in the region, and a big reason was their benefactor, a rancher and oilman Robert O. Anderson. The former wildcatter began his career with skillful investment at 24 years of age, and he consolidated his wells into the renowned Atlantic Richfield Company. After meeting the artists in the 1950s, Anderson assumed the same role the Medici Family had in Italy. He was the patron that energized museums, preservation, and the artists that created them.[368]

If Robert O. Anderson was the engine, John Meigs fueled the enthusiasm for Lincoln preservation. The artist gathered like-minded friends such as author Paul Horgan and mentor Peter Hurd. With Anderson on board, San Patricio served as headquarters for a new private-funded endeavor, the Lincoln County Historical Trust. Although planning took over a year, newspapers announced its formation in April 1977. Meigs emerged its leader, and he extolled its eventual goals spread to other media ventures such as publishing. One paragraph summed up their mission: *"The purpose of the Lincoln County Heritage Trust is to investigate the possibilities of preservation and public admission to these properties on a non-profit basis."*[369]

Meigs, as Executive Director, guided the Trust directly into the path of the ailing Old Lincoln County Historical Commission. They snapped up property in the town that the Commission could not afford, such as the Montano Store, in hopes of setting a "one admission" ticket for visitors. The state government controlled the underfunded Commission, and they realized the money in the Trust funded Lincoln's future. With reduced influence, the obsolete Commission was "reorganized" out of existence in the summer of 1979.[370] The Museum of New Mexico, who controlled numerous exhibits throughout the state, became a separate agency. An agreement was reached between the Trust and the Museum in July, and the Trust acquisitions moved to state control. With his usual bombast, Meigs proclaimed victory for Lincoln.

Now that the Museum of New Mexico has been established as a separate state agency with an interest in the Lincoln properties and a strong citizen group is operating to preserve the unique character of Lincoln and the valley. The Trust feels its mission has been accomplished and is pleased to relinquish the lease.[371]

Although Meigs moved on to other interests, one person never could move on. By 1976, William Morrison felt left behind. A decade after his pivotal role in the Telfer case, he gathered his papers and deposited them at the Illinois State Historical Library. This collection was primarily composed of family history, as his notes were lost for a number of years. The most important loss was those of the Brushy Bill period.[372]

The epitaph to William Morrison's historical adventures was found in two letters. The first of these was written to his longtime friend and co-author, Leland Sonnichsen, on March 28, 1977. The tone was evidence that some of the old fight remained in him. *"I have been destroying files for years and started again recently,"* he wrote in his opening line. He ruminated about his personal insights over his past actions. For example, Morrison burned a contract regarding their book and was relying on a rejected document when discussing terms with his co-author for *Alias Billy the Kid.* He commended Mullin, adding his *"integrity was unquestionable."* He saved his venom for the late William Keleher, who passed away in 1972. Morrison took issue with a photostatic copy of "the faked Jury Verdict" published in the former commissioner's *Violence in Lincoln County.* Additionally, he railed about changes edited from his research findings and how it affected copyright law.[373]

The second Morrison letter was written on December 14, 1976 to Barbara Franklin at the University of New Mexico. It clarified the later communication to Sonnichsen. A request for photographs associated with *Alias Billy the Kid*, intended for a magazine article, prompted the letters to both Franklin and Sonnichsen. Morrison snubbed the request, while Sonnichsen did not object. He wrote Franklin that the requestor wanted one photograph from the book and a number not included in it, and he considered a buyout of Sonnichsen's interest in the publication. Morrison's real intent was buried in the text of the letter.

I feel that I should report scientific findings in the matter of the Kid in a new work for the purpose of dispelling fiction put forth as fact. Historians have little, if any, interest in fact supported by evidence...I have been thinking, as mentioned before, to offer to purchase the interest of Dr. Sonnichsen, and requesting the Press to reconvey the copyright as specified in our agreement executed on the 3rd day of June, 1954 [pen or pencil corrected a typed "5"], with Mr. Mann, to which reference is hereby made for clarification.[374]

Whatever his plans may have been, William Morrison died before he acted on them. In August 1977, the 70-year-old former bankruptcy referee for the federal district court passed away in El Paso. Although complex and impatient, the diligent researcher gathered like-minded followers in his philosophy. In Roswell, citizens William Tunstill and Kenneth Osthimer formed an interest group called the "Billy 'THE KID' Research Committee." Tunstill, who authored several limited editions of titles that raised eyebrows—*Jesse James Was One of My Names* (1975) and *Billy the Kid and Me Were the Same* (1988). Tunstill and his contemporaries pursued a number of extensive historical theories well into the 1980s, proving that Billy the Kid remained in the minds of Americans for some time.[375]

The death of Morrison ended the vestiges of historical tumult initiated with the Telfer Case. However, tombstone thieves again struck the Old Fort Cemetery in February 1981. Hooligans made off with the 100-pound stone in broad daylight. The ranger at the state monument office was not surprised, and he called it a "publicity ploy" for the 100th anniversary of the Kid's death. The whole episode lasted about a week. An anonymous caller tipped off state police that the marker was in a Huntington Beach, California residence. Police found the tombstone, and De Baca County Sheriff John McBride flew out to retrieve it. An airline kindly flew the weighty icon back free of charge. Oddly, while the 1940 stone was stolen twice, there was no known attempt to dig up the Kid's body during this period.[376]

The second Billy the Kid tombstone theft probably did not surprise Lois Telfer, but she never publicly spoke of it again. Since the mid-1960s, few publications made more than a passing mention of her quest to move the body to Lincoln. She lived quietly in New York until her death. Unlike the press she received as a society child and as a relative of the Kid, her end was barely noticed. A brief mention was found in the *Bronx Press Review* of September 1, 1983. A service was held at the Thomas C. Montera Funeral Home, followed by a burial in New York's Mount Hope Cemetery. She was survived by no immediate relatives, save distant cousins.[377]

While few surviving participants from the Lois Telfer hearings outlived her, a few lived on. Proud of his work in the Billy the Kid case and his fondness for Fort Sumner, John Humphrey eventually moved to Lovington, New Mexico. His daughter Myrl Jane noted that he built a home and took up gardening. After six years in Lovington, he suffered a stroke. He lived the remainder of his life in a nursing home, dying in January 1995. In Lincoln, Roman Maes survived both the case and the Boylans. Maes resisted the Lincoln County Historical Trust in the late 1970s and independently operated the La Paloma Museum well into the next decade. The *Roswell Daily Record* featured the couple and their museum in a July 1985 article. They charged a dollar for admission at the door, and Roman and Theodora shared their collections and stories. Tourism dollars, augmented by social security, allowed them to "get by," she stated. With Roman's death in September 1989, the museum closed and its contents auctioned.[378]

The arts community thrived in Lincoln County long after John Meigs headed the Lincoln County Historical Trust. However, the contingent thinned over time. Peter Hurd, the leading light of the colorful landscape, died in July 1984. His wife Henriette Wyeth Hurd painted former First Lady Patricia Nixon and likewise earned laurels. After Peter's death, Henriette continued her work until her own passing in April 1997. Despite his appearance, their neighbor Meigs never achieved great wealth. After losing his adopted son, Clifton, to a heart condition in 1989, his restless spirit whirled in various forms of art media. He spent lavishly on projects. He even built a pantheon at Fort Meigs in preparation for his own death and burial. That occurred on August 29, 2003, years after he donated his home to a Benedictine monastery. Even in death, John Liggett Meigs proved expensive.[379]

Louis Bowdre died on December 30, 2004. There appeared to be a public aversion to the subject, as his obituary never noted the hearing. Neither did an interview he did with a Bartlesville, Oklahoma newspaper in July 2002. When Lincoln County re-opened the Billy the Kid case the previous year, there were again fears of digging for the Kid's body. Town officials scrambled with panic to prevent a repeat of the events four decades past. Opponents of the case thought of contacting Bowdre, but it was too late. The old postman passed away amid a slew of newspaper articles on the new case.[380]

The last survivors of the series of events in 1961-62 lived in Lincoln County. Lloyd Davis thrived in business in Ruidoso. He died on March 5, 2016. Joe Sargent's widow, Sharon, recovered from the blast that killed her husband. Within a few years, she remarried to Eugene Degner and moved to Alamogordo, New Mexico. As the 60th anniversary of the Telfer hearing nears, the memories are almost completely faded.[381]

The story ended where it started. Betty Grabbe, the great-grandniece of Charlie Bowdre, was surprised when she learned of the trial—and had no idea who Louis Bowdre was. In fact, the Bowdre family knew Charlie's fate, but there was no apparent involvement. How then did Assistant District Attorney Humphrey find Louis Bowdre as "next of kin"? The same questions applied to Lois Telfer's claim as "next of kin" to Billy the Kid. Given these facts disprove the crucial pillars of the case, there's an open question if the legal proceedings of the 1961-62 war between De Baca and Lincoln Counties were even valid. ? Perhaps it does not matter. Judge Hensley was correct about one thing—no one could locate the body of Billy the Kid without risk of accidently disturbing the remains of another grave. Whether he's in the grounds of the Old

Fort Cemetery or elsewhere, Billy the Kid lies buried in American history. He's staying there.[382]

[1] J. Vernon Smithson, comp., <u>Billy the Kid's Grave</u>, Works Progress Administration (WPA) Files, New Mexico Points of Interest, April 21, 1936, Manuscript Division, Library of Congress. These are considered federal government records from the New Deal Era. The National Archives houses their administrative files in Record Group 69.

[2] Ibid.

[3] Marc Simmons, "Grave in Shackles," *Santa Fe Reporter,* October 3, 1982; Lillie Gerhardt Anderson, "Historic Fort Sumner," *New Mexico Magazine*, November 1952, 18-19; *Albuquerque Journal*, November 17, 1961; Notes, "Bonney Grave, Ft. Sumner," Robert N. Mullin Collection, Haley Memorial Library and History Center, Midland, Texas; Grady E. McCright, "Who Sleeps in Billy the Kid's Tomb?" *True Frontier*, April 1978, 12-13.

[4] "Coroner's Report Proves Billy the Kid Is Dead, Historian Asserts," *El Paso Times*, August 5, 1951; <u>Kid's Grave</u>, from *Las Vegas Optic,* January 16, 1882; Charles Dudrow, Sketch of Fort Sumner Cemetery, RG 393, Records of United States Army Continental Commands, 1821-1920, National Archives and Records Administration. The mention of sidewalk placement was made during the author's visit to the cemetery.

[5] John W. Poe, *The Death of Billy the Kid* (Boston and New York: Houghton Mifflin Company, 1933), 41-42

[6] Ibid., 42-43.

[7] Ibid., 45.

[8] Ibid., 56-58. The Spanish version immediately precedes the English translation.

[9] Joe Bowlin, "The Anaya Document," in A.P. "Paco" Anaya, *I Buried Billy* (College Station, Texas: Creative Publishing Company, 1991), 10-11; James H. Earle, "Editor's Preface," in Anaya, *I Buried Billy*, 17-19; "Critique of Burns," in Anaya, *I Buried* Billy, 142-146; Walter Noble Burns, *The Saga of Billly the Kid* (New York: Grosset & Dunlap, 1926); Walter Noble Burns to Maurice Fulton, January 21 [ca. 1928], Maurice Garland Fulton Collection, University of Arizona Special Collections. Fulton was working on a second edition of Patrick F. Garrett's *Authentic Life of Billy the Kid*, and apparently took Burns to task over an article. He was defensive in his response to Fulton, claiming his work was "very careful and painstaking...In gathering my data I spent three months driving all over New Mexico interviewing persons who had part in the Lincoln County war [sic] and knew the Kid intimately and had first hand and often eye-witness information..."

[10] Anaya, *I Buried Billy*, 132. See page 142-146 for his critique of Burns.

[11] Ibid.

[12] Ibid., 133; James H. Earle, Editor's Preface, in *I Buried Billy*, 17.

[13] "Says Pete Maxwell-I Had Three Chances to be Killed," *Tinnie's Historical Roundup*, July 1981, Volume III, Number 3, 1; "Searches for Marker from Grave of Billy the Kid," *Clovis News-Journal*, May 19, 1934.

[14] "Removal Attempt Made in 1925," *Lincoln County News*, May 12, 1961.

[15] Maurice G. Fulton, comp., Jack Potter, "The Grave of Billy the Kid and Its Marker," Undated, Dolph Briscoe Center for American History, The University of Texas Special Collections at Austin, Texas; See also, "Searches for Marker from Grave of Billy the Kid," *Clovis News-Journal*, May 19, 1934.

[16] "Bonney Grave, Ft. Sumner." in Robert N. Mullin Collection, Haley Memorial Library and History Center, Midland, Texas.

[17] Ibid.

[18] A number of Jack Potter's articles were compiled and published as Col. Jack Potter, *Cattle Trails of the Old West* (Clayton, NM: Laura R. Krehbiel, 1935 and 1939). After Potter's death in 1950, the bulk of his papers were deposited at Eastern New Mexico University in Portales, New Mexico—but some were scattered in other institutions. An excellent biography that features some of his stories is Jean M. Burroughs, *On the Trail-The Life and Tales of "Lead Steer" Potter* (Santa Fe, NM: Museum of New Mexico Press, 1980).

[19] "City to Mark Grave of 'Billy the Kid," *El Paso Herald-Post*, July 8, 1930.

[20] Ibid.

[21] Flyer, Mrs. Adelina J. Welborn, *"Requescate en Pacem,"* Morgue File, Fort Sumner, Historical Society for Southeast New Mexico.

[22] James N. Warner to Mrs. R.A. Doak, April 6, 1940, MSS 3079, Special Collections, History Colorado. This was formerly known as the Colorado Historical Society.

[23] "The Kid's Stone Brought Home," *Clovis News-Journal*, June 3, 1976.

[24] Ibid.

[25] Entry, Charles S. Meriwether to Albert R. Bowdre, DeWitt County Deeds, 411; Ancestry.com. *U.S., Find A Grave Index, 1600s-Current* [database on-line]. Provo, UT, USA: Ancestry.com Operations, Inc., 2012; Tombstones, located on private property, Senatobia, Mississippi.

[26] Ibid.; 1870 United States Federal Census, Population Schedules, DeSoto County, Mississippi, RG29, M593, Roll 728, Page 334B, National Archives and Records Administration [NARA], n.d.; 1880 United States Federal Census, Population Schedules, Tate County, Mississippi, RG29, M593, Roll 665, Page 299D, NARA, n.d.; email, Betty Grabbe to Author, July 9, 2012; email, Betty Grabbe to Author, July 13, 2012.

[27] *DeSoto [MS] Times*, April 7, 1932. Additional information provided by the family.

[28] Robert Mullin noted that Postmaster G.W. Bailey of Silver City, New Mexico Territory had two "uncalled for mail lists," dated April 12 and October 1, 1873, which listed "Charles Bowdre" or "Blowdre." Robert N. Mullin Collection, Haley Memorial Library and History Center, Midland, Texas; Notes, 1959-032 Donald

Cline Collection of New Mexico Research Materials, Collection 10418, New Mexico State Archives, Santa Fe, New Mexico.

[29] Interview, Mike and Harold Stewart, Eastland, Texas, January 10, 2009. This took place during the Scurlock Reunion at this time.

[30] Ibid.

[31] Notes, "Voter Registration," 1959-032 Donald Cline Collection of New Mexico Materials, Collection 10418, Folder 10, New Mexico State Archives; Notes, "Lincoln County Poll Book, Nov. 1876, Pct. 3," 1959-032 Donald Cline Collection of New Mexico Research Materials, Collection 10418, Folder 10, New Mexico State Archives.

[32] Ed Bartholomew, *Jesse Evans-A Texas Hide-Burner* (Houston, TX: Frontier Press of Texas, 1955), 20; Notes on "Charley Bowdre" in Robert N. Mullin Collection, Haley Memorial Library and History Center, Midland, Texas.

[33] Ibid. Note that the spelling of "Jesse" was sometimes "Jessie" Evans.

[34] Bartholomew, *Jesse Evans*, 20, as taken from Notes on "Charley Bowdre" in Mullin Collection, Haley Memorial Library, Midland, Texas.

[35] Philip J. Rasch, Joseph E. Buckbee, and Karl K. Klein, "Man of Many Parts," in Barry C. Johnson, Ed., *English Westerners' Brand Book*, Vol. 5, No. 2, January 1963, 10. This is also found in Robert K. DeArment, ed., *Trailing Billy the Kid* (Stillwater, OK: National Association for Outlaw and Lawman History, Inc., 1995), 89-99.

[36] Notes, "Communication on Attempt to Murder John S. Chisum," from *Mesilla Independent*, August 1877, in Maurice G. Fulton Papers (MS 057), Box 10, Folder 10, Special Collections, University of Arizona Libraries.

[37] Notes, "Communication," August 17, 1877 unnamed account, in Fulton Papers (MS 057).

[38] Notes, "Communication," *Mesilla Independent*, August 1877, in Fulton Papers (MS 057).

[39] Notes, "Communication," Unnamed account, in Fulton Papers; Rasch, Buckbee, and Klein, "Man of Many Parts," in Barry C. Johnson, Ed., *English Westerners' Brand Book*, Vol. 5, No. 2, January 1963, 10.

[40] Notes, "Charley Bowdre," in Mullin Collection, Haley Memorial Library; Corn Exchange Hotel Register, John Davis, Proprietor, September 22, 1877, Copy Courtesy of Steve Sederwall, Capitan, New Mexico.

[41] Rasch, Buckbee, and Klein, "Man of Many Parts," in Barry C. Johnson, Ed., *English Westerners' Brand Book*, Vol. 5, No. 2, January 1963, 10; Glenn Dodson, "Ranch house more of a fortress than a home," *Houston Chronicle*, January 1, 2008; Typed Notes, "Charges in Lincoln County Against Participants in Lincoln County War," in 1959-032 Donald Cline Collection of New Mexico Materials, Collection 10418, Folder 11, New Mexico State Archives.

[42] Rasch, Buckbee, and Klein, "Man of Many Parts," in Barry C. Johnson, Ed., *English Westerners' Brand Book*, Vol. 5, No. 2, January 1963, 10.

[43] Robert N. Mullin, ed., *Maurice Garland Fulton's History of the Lincoln County War* (Tucson, AZ: University of Arizona Press, 1967), 115-117; Ibid., 137-141. See also David S. Turk, *Blackwater Draw* (Santa Fe, NM: Sunstone Press, 2011).

[44] Mullin, ed., *Fulton's History*, 141; Maurice G. Fulton, *Roswell In Its Early Years* (Roswell, NM: Hall-Poorbaugh Press, Inc., 1963), 28.

[45] Mullin, ed., *Fulton's History,* 158-159.

[46] Mullin, ed., *Fulton's History*, 172-175; Transcript, "Public Meeting held at Mescalero, New Mexico, Sunday afternoon, June 12, 1932, under the Auspices of the Alamogordo Chamber of Commerce," 7, in Blazer Family Papers (MS 034), Box 1, Folder 11, Special Collections, University of Arizona Libraries. Much of the Coe version was later retold in his memoir of events, known as *Frontier Fighter* (1934).

[47] Transcript, "Public Meeting," June 12, 1932, 1, in Blazer Family Papers (MS 034), Box 1, Folder 11, Special Collections, University of Arizona Special Collections.

[48] Ibid., 7. Tinnie is the reference to a village east of San Patricio, New Mexico. It is approximately 20 miles east of Lincoln. The "cousin" referenced is Frank Coe, who lived in the area.

[49] Ibid., 8.

[50] Ibid., 8-9.

[51] Ibid., 9. Blazer and George Coe were both speaking at this time.

[52] Rich Eastwood, *Nuestras Madres-A Story of Lincoln County New Mexico* (Author, Undated), 88. From a collection "A Family of the West," by Rich Eastwood, Version 09.03.22. This is a full publication of genealogy and family accounts.

[53] Interview, Mike and Harold Stewart, Eastland, Texas, January 10, 2009.

[54] Ibid.; Eastwood, *Nuestras Madres-A Story of Lincoln County New Mexico,* 91-92.

[55] Email, Betty Grabbe to Author, July 13, 2012.

[56] Ibid.; EMail, Betty Grabbe to Author, July 9, 2012.

[57] Rasch, Buckbee, and Klein, "Man of Many Parts," in Johnson, Ed., *English Westerners' Society*, Vol. 5, No. 2, January 1963, 11; Bartholomew, *Jesse Evans,* 20, as taken from Notes on "Charley Bowdre" in Mullin Collection, Haley Memorial Library and History Center, Midland, Texas; Robert N. Mullin, ed., *Fulton's History*, 213-215.

[58] Rasch, Buckbee, and Klein, "Man of Many Parts," in Johnson, Ed., *English Westerners' Society*, Vol. 5, No. 2, January 1963, 11.

[59] Ibid., 11-12.

[60] Ibid., 12; Mullin, ed., *Fulton's History*, 286-287.

[61] Typed Notes, taken from "[Miguel] OTERO—The Real Billy the Kid," Ramon Adams Collection, MA82-6, Box 11, Folder 3, Dallas Public Library; Entry of H.A. Smith, Petra and Jose Valdez, Tenth Census of the United States, 1880 (Washington, D.C., National Archives and Records Administration), San Miguel

County, New Mexico [Terr.], Roll 803, Image 838;   Louis Leon Branch, *"Los Bilitos": The Story of "Billy the Kid" and his Gang-As told by Charles Frederick Rudolph-a member of Garrett's historical posse* (New York: Hearthstone Books, Carlton Press, Inc., 1980), 209.

[62] Jeff C. Dykes, *Law on a Wild Frontier*, GREAT WESTERN Series No. 5 (Potomac Corral of the Westerners, Washington, D.C., May 1969), 8-9.

[63] Donald R. Lavash, "Thomas G. Yerby and Nasaria," The Outlaw Gazette (Taiban, NM: Billy the Kid Outlaw Gang, December 1992, Vol V, No. 1), 10-11.

[64] Lavash, "Thomas G. Yerby,"*Outlaw Gazette,* December 1992, 10-11.

[65] Ibid.; Mullin, ed., Maurice Garland Fulton's History, 249; Notes, "Garrett Now Sheriff," Robert N. Mullin Collection, Haley Memorial Library and History Center, Midland, Texas.

[66] Email, Harold Stewart to Author, October 30, 2012.

[67] Interview, Mike and Harold Stewart, January 10, 2009, Eastland, Texas; Texas Department of Health, Bureau of Vital Statistics, Certificate of Death, J.G. Scurlock, No. 34767.

[68] Donald R. Lavash, *Wilson and the Kid* (College Station, TX: Creative Publishing Co., 1990), 32; Henry F. Hoyt, *A Frontier Doctor* (Boston and New York: Houghton Mifflin Company: The Riverside Press Cambridge, 1929), 110-113.

[69] Lavash,"Thomas G. Yerby," *Outlaw Gazette,* December 1992, 10-11; Louis Leon Branch, *"Los Bilitos,"* 144.

[70] Branch. *"Los Bilitos."* 163-164; Mullin. ed.. *Maurice Garland Fulton's History of the Lincoln County War*, 372. Sunnyside was the hamlet that later became the town of Fort Sumter.

[71] Ibid.

[72] "Charlie Bowdre's Last Letter," in Peter Hertzog, *Little Known Facts About Billy, the Kid*, No. 3 (Santa Fe, NM: Press of the Territorian, 1964); Application for Pension, D.M. Dockery, September 19, 1929, Mississippi Office of the State Auditor, Mississippi Department of Archives and History. Charlie drew the line at rustling, and a later message from Jose Valdez to Dockery after his death proved the family had not completely isolated him.

[73] Email, Betty Grabbe to Author, July 13, 2012. She was quoting her cousin Paul Bowdre, who lives in Georgia.

[74] Lavash, *Wilson and the Kid*, 51-52; Ibid., 54-55; Julie Carter, "Counterfeit note rewrites chapter of Billy the Kid," *Ruidoso News*, July 16, 2010.

[75] F. Stanley, *Desperadoes of New Mexico* (Denver, Colorado: World Press, Inc., 1953), 179. Father Stanley Crocchiola (1908-1996) was a New Yorker who moved to Texas and New Mexico and wrote over 150 local histories.

[76] Entries of September 21 and October 4-5, 1880, Reports of Azariah F. Wild, Special Operative, U.S. Treasury Department, Secret Service Division, Record Group 87, National Archives and Records Administration (NARA); Entries of October 4-5, October 6, and October 10, 1880, Wild Reports, Secret Service Division, RG87, NARA.

[77] Entries of October 8 and 10, 1880, Wild Reports, Secret Service Division, RG87, NARA; Harold L. Edwards, "Barney Mason-In the Shadow of Pat Garrett and Billy the Kid," *Old West*, Summer 1990, 15. Wild's entry of October 21, 1880 revealed his "Posse Comitatus" had 30 men at that time. Entries of October 6, 18, and 21, 1880, Wild Reports, RG87, NARA. By October 29, Wild concluded this was "W.H. West" and not "James." This was most likely an alias for using the name of William Harvey West, who was an employee of Charles Rath, the famous buffalo hunter and salesman. There is conjecture over this man's real identity. One was a known counterfeiter named William Budd, and another a sharper known as Frank Doyle. The latter was the brother of a counterfeit connection in Illinois, James Doyle. The plates actually originated in New York with the famous "Prince of Counterfeiters" William Brockway.

[78] Entry of October 19, 1880, Wild Reports, RG87, NARA.

[79] Entries of October 9, 16, 18, 19, and 21, 1880, Wild Reports, RG87, NARA; Lavash, "Thomas G. Yerby," *Outlaw Gazette*, December 1992, 11. "DeVours" claimed to be part of the ring himself. While it's possible this was a cover for Mason, it might have been a local man named Doerges.

[80] Entries of October 21, 29 and November 2, 1880, Wild Reports, RG87, NARA; Lavash, "Thomas G. Yerby," *Outlaw Gazette*, December 1992, 11.

[81] Entries of October 31, November 1, 8 and 11, 1880, Wild Reports, RG87, NARA.

[82] Entries of November 8, 11, and 21, 1880, Wild Reports, RG87, NARA; Edwards, "Barney Mason-In the Shadow of Pat Garrett and Billy the Kid," *Old West*, Summer 1990, 15-16.

[83] Edwards, "Barney Mason-In the Shadow of Pat Garrett and Billy the Kid," *Old West*, Summer 1990, 15-16; Lavash, "Thomas G. Yerby," *Outlaw Gazette*, December 1992, 11.

[84] Ibid.

[85] John P. Wilson, ed., *Pat Garrett and Billy the Kid as I Knew Them-Reminiscences of John P. Meadows* (Albuquerque, NM: University of New Mexico Press, 2004), 43; Ibid., 156. Wilson published the first book-sized account of newspaper pieces and manuscripts of Meadows. According to Wilson, the primary manuscript (a copy was typed by Fulton) was in the papers of historian Philip Rasch at the Lincoln State Monument.

[86] Quote from *Pat Garrett and Billy the Kid as I Knew Them: Reminscences of John P. Meadows* edited by John P. Wilson. Copyright @2004 ed., University of New Mexico Press, 2004, 43-44.

[87] Ibid.

[88] Entry of December 4, 1880, Wild Reports, RG87, NARA. Note that in the 1880 Federal Census that J.C. Lea's brother Frank lived close to the livery stable in White Oaks. He moved his family from there, but it leaves the possibility that the Leas might have known quite a lot more about the actual operation or simply drew the conclusion that Wilson was the leader. Historian Don Lavash's notes

highlight this event as "important!!" It might be noted Lavash's work, *Wilson and the Kid*, strongly indicates that Billy Wilson was set up as well.

[89] Phil Cooke to Robert Mullin, September 14, 1964, Philip Cooke III Collection, New Mexico State Archives, Santa Fe, New Mexico. Cooke is referring to a book by Peter Hertzog, *Little Known Facts about Billy, the Kid,* published by the Press of the Territorian and copyrighted by Cooke that year. Bowdre's final letter was published in full within it, on pages 14 through 16. Notation by Hertzog in that text credits the Huntington Library, San Marino, California.

[90] "Charlie Bowdre's Letter," in Mullin Collection, Haley Library & Memorial Archives. This was a typed copy of the original letter. See also "Charlie Bowdre's Last Letter," in Hertzog, Little Known Facts, 14-16.

[91] Branch, *"Los Bilitos,"* 208-209.

[92] Ibid., 209-210. Rudolph's account is one of the most detailed descriptions of Thomas O'Folliard's death. Supposedly Barney Mason told O'Folliard to "take your medicine like a man."

[93] Ibid., 210-211. See also James H. Earle, ed., *The Capture of Billy the Kid* (College Station, TX: Creative Publishing Co., 1988), 104-105.

[94] Branch, *"Los Bilitos,"* 210.

[95] Ibid., 212.

[96] Ethel C. Dulaney, comp., "Louis Bousman," Works Progress Administration (WPA) Interview Files, Manuscript Division, Library of Congress.

[97] Ibid., Branch, *"Los Dilitos,"* 212.

[98] Dulaney, comp., "Louis Bousman," Works Progress Administration Interview Files, Manuscript Division, Library of Congress.

[99] Ibid.

[100] Bill Kelly, "Bowdre Mystery Yet to be Laid to Rest," *New Mexico Magazine*, February 1993, 33-34. Kelly's source on Coe taking Bowdre's body appears to be someone named "Iris Bowdre" of New Jersey, who write him in 1961. This corresponds with the Telfer petition and remains unverified. "Iris" also claimed to be Bowdre's closest living relative, which was absolutely false. However, as Telfer made this claim with the Kid, there might be confusion with her.

[101] Jeff C. Dykes, *Law on a Wild Frontier-Four Sheriffs of Lincoln County* (Washington, D.C.: Potomac Corral, The Westerners, May 1969), 11-14; Typed Notes, "Billy Leaves Las Vegas for Santa Fe Jail (2nd interview) Dec. 28, 1880. By George Fitzpatrick," Don Lavash Papers, Copy with Author.

[102] Dykes, *Law on a Wild Frontier,* 11-14.

[103] Dulaney, comp., "Louis Bousman," Works Progress Administration Interview Files, Manuscript Division, Library of Congress; Dykes, *Law on a Wild Frontier*, 14-15.

[104] Dulaney, comp., "Louis Bousman," Works Progress Administration Interview Files, Manuscript Division, Library of Congress; Branch, *"Los Bilitos,"* 250-251; William V. Morrison to Paul Baker, May 14, 1961, Blazer Collection, University of Arizona Special Collections, Tucson, Arizona, Box 1, Folder 10.

[105] J.L. Valdez to Mr. D.M. Dockery, Jan 16/80 [81], Copy, from Scott Emerson, Hernando, Mississippi. This letter has remained inside the family until provided a copy by the request of the author and Mr. Emerson's relative, Betty Grabbe.

[106] Ibid. The alliteration has been carefully observed in this letter, which has a mixture of misspellings and odd phrasings.

[107] Ibid.; Branch, "Los Bilitos," 209. Valdez and Campbell were two of the Kid's known friends in the Fort Sumner area. It was said Garrett threatened Valdez at gunpoint on the letter to lure the Kid and his gang back to town.

[108] Donald R. Lavash to William A. Tunstill, May 5, 1982. Copy in possession of author.

[109] Maurice Fulton to Robert N. Mullin, July 4, 1953, Mullin Collection, Haley Memorial Library and History Center, Midland, Texas.

[110] Louis F. Rudulph [Rudolph] Jr. to Donald R. Lavash, 4 October 85. Copy of typed letter in possession of author. Keleher's name is incorrectly spelled.

[111] "Coroner's Report Proves Billy the Kid Is Dead, Historian Asserts," El Paso Times, August 5, 1951; William V. Morrison to George Fitzpatrick, February 24, 1951, MSS 3096, Eve Ball papers, 20th Century Western and Mormon Manuscripts, L. Tom Perry Special Collections, Harold B. Lee Library, Brigham Young University, Box 26, Folder 6.

[112] Copy, Typed Letter, Maurice G. Fulton to J.C. [Jeff] Dykes, 16 July 1952, Jeff Dykes Collection, Cushing Memorial Library and Archives, Texas A&M University, College Station, TX.

[113] "Says Pete Maxwell-I Had Three Chances to be Killed," Tinnie's Historical Roundup, July 1981, Volume III, No. 3, 1. From the writings of Jack Potter; Notes,"Billy Death," Robert N. Mullin Collection, Haley Memorial Library and History Center, Midland, Texas. From Walter Noble Burns' research for Saga of Billy the Kid. Note that Burns was incorrect in the surname of the Fort Sumner citizen who built the coffin.

[114] Notes from Felisita Swerbecker Sandoval, from Author's Collection. The author obtained this information from the Old Fort Sumner Museum, and purchased the tintype of A.P. "Paco" Anaya, which also contained descriptive information on the burial ceremonies.

[115] John P. Wilson, "With His Boots Off: First Newspaper Reports on the Death of Billy the Kid," Rio Grande History, No. 14, 1983, 11-12.

[116] Ibid., 12.

[117] "Ranchero," Las Vegas Daily Optic, July 18, 1881, as printed in Wilson, "With His Boots Off."

[118] Ibid.

[119] Ibid.

[120] "Clayton, N.M. Pioneer in Quest of Grave Marker of "Billy the Kid." Thinks it may be in a Museum," Trinidad Chronicle News, May 19, 1934.

[121] Ibid. Paco Anaya's story would later be published as I Buried Billy after the Brushy Bill Roberts claim.

[132] John Roark to Jack Potter, May 17, 1930, Bacon Papers, 51057303, Western History and Genealogy Department, The Denver Public Library.

[133] Potter pursued the fate of the marker for several years. Eventually he heard back from Theodore S. Woolsey's sister Edith in April 1930, but nothing was learned. A piece of the original marker surfaced in Missouri and was later placed in the Old Fort Sumner Museum. This was likely taken before the marker was removed.

[134] McAlavy and Kilmer, *High Plains History*, 6; Ibid., 9; Alfred T. Bacon to Theodore S. Woolsey, July 23, 1886, Bacon Papers, 51057303, Western History and Genealogy Department, The Denver Public Library.

[135] McAlavy and Kilmer, *High Plains History*, 6; Copy, Bill of Sale from Thomas G. Yerby to the New England Live Stock Company, Bill of Sale Docket 1881-89, Lincoln County, 191-192; Lavash, "Thomas G. Yerby," *Outlaw Gazette,* December 1992, 11; Copy, M.S. Brazil to M[anuel] Abreu Esq., February 13, 1892, obtained from Abreu Family; McAlavy and Kilmer, *High Plains History*, 17. Yerby moved to Colorado and married a woman 20 years his junior. They had 7 children. He and his family moved to Sarasota, Florida for some years, and finally moved to Sacramento, California, where he died on October 14, 1941 at the age of 94. Information from Robin Tidmore to Author, April 6, 2012.

[136] McAlavy and Kilmer, *High Plains History*, 48; "Death of Lonny Horn," *Rocky Mountain News*, March 8, 1903; Alfred T. Bacon to Nathaniel T. Bacon Esq., December 20, 1892, Bacon Family Papers, Rhode Island Historical Society; Alfred T. Bacon to W.T. Bacon, August 9, 1894, Bacon Family Papers, Rhode Island Historical Society; *Denver Times*, June 5, 1901.

[137] *Albuquerque Journal*, November 17, 1961; Typed Notes, "Bonney Grave, Ft Sumner," Robert N. Mullin Collection, Haley Memorial Library and History Center, Midland, Texas; "Fort Sumner Cemetery Bodies to be Removed to the National One at Santa Fe," *Deseret Evening News*, December 16, 1905; "Twenty-Two Soldier Bodies Removed," *Albuquerque Citizen*, March 3, 1906. A further flood devastated the grounds in 1941, washing away a portion of the adobe structures of the former fort.

[138] Interview, Nellie Ruth Jones, Glencoe, New Mexico, October 16, 2013.

[139] Ibid.

[140] *Historical Reminiscences and Biographical Memoirs of Conway County, Arkansas* (Little Rock: Arkansas Historical Publishing Company, 1890), 39; Epsey Bowdre Morgan Cooke (Mrs. Robert P. Cooke, Jr.) to Mr. Hillard, August 26, 1972, Payne Subject File, Mississippi State Archives, Jackson, Mississippi. Plumerville was formerly spelled "Plummerville," for Samuel Plummer, the original landowner. The town was named in 1874.

[141] Anderson, "Historic Fort Sumner," *New Mexico*, 18-19; "Bonney Grave, Ft. Sumner," Mullin Collection, Haley Memorial Library and History Center, Midland, Texas. The location of the cemetery moved to higher ground in 1920.

[142] "50 Years Ago," *Albuquerque Journal,* January 26, 1967; "Governor Debaca Dead," *Buffalo Morning News and Illustrated Buffalo Express,* February 19, 1917; Burns, *The Saga of Billy the Kid;* Maurice Fulton, ed., of Garrett, *The Authentic History of Billy the Kid* (New York: MacMillan Company, 1927). See the late Paul Dworkin's study of Burns, *American Mythmaker-Walter Noble Burns and the Legends of Billy the Kid, Wyatt Earp and Joaquin Murrieta* (Norman, OK: University of Oklahoma Press, 2015).

[143] There were a number of factors in the disparity of accessibility in this early period, but weather and flood conditions of the Pecos during this period contributed. In later years, once the interstate highway system bypassed Fort Sumner (but also did the same with Lincoln), it permanently cost the hamlet a good percentage of visitation. However, several museums and regional interest helped.

[144] C.L. Sonnichsen and William V. Morrison, *Alias Billy the Kid* (Barto, PA: Creative Texts Publishers, 2014), 13-16; Ibid., 20-21. Morrison began his case in 1948. By 1950, it was nationwide news.

[145] Sonnichsen and Morrison, *Alias Billy the Kid* (Albuquerque, NM: University of New Mexico Press, 1955) ; Biographical Description in, "William V. Morrison," in Manuscript Acquisitions, with memorandum from Paul D. Spence, Curator of Manuscripts, to Morrison, March 9, 1973, Illinois State Historical Society, as copied in Eve Ball Papers, 1855-1984, MS3090, Box 26, Folder 6, Brigham Young University. Morrison placed a good amount of his papers in the library of the Illinois Historical Society, which described his ancestor as the sibling of Lucien Bonaparte Maxwell. Spence noted in Manuscript Acquisitions, Page 92: "The material centers primarily on Morrison's research to establish the heirship of Peter Menard. This research was begun in 1925 by Morrison and P. Menard Maxwell in Taos, New Mexico, and culminated in a 1942-43 civil suit to recover 2,943 acres of Menard land."

[146] *Las Vegas Daily Optic,* June 24, 1898; H.S. Hunter, "Collect Funds for Monument at Grave of 'Billy the Kid.' October 15, 1928.

[147] Handbill, "Requescate en Pacem," Morgue File, Fort Sumner, Historical Society for Southeast New Mexico. This handbill was found loose in the file.

[148] *Albuquerque Journal,* November 17, 1961.

[149] "City to Mark Grave of 'Billy the Kid,' *El Paso Herald-Post,* July 8, 1930; *Albuquerque Journal,* January 25, 1962. Perkins recalled that two of the witnesses approached him. This had to be Silva and Anaya, as Charles Foor arrived in Fort Sumner in 1883, two years after the Kid's death.

[150] J. Vernon Smithson, "Billy the Kid's Grave," WPA Files, Manuscript Division, Library of Congress.

[151] J. Vernon Smithson, "Points of Interest," "Billy the Kid's Museum," WPA Files, May 11, 1936, Manuscripts Division, Library of Congress; Copy of Description, Photo 6.6, File B, Series IV, Robert N. Mullin Collection, Haley Library and Research Center, Midland, Texas.

[152] Wilbur F. Coe, *Ranch on the Ruidoso, the Story of a Pioneer Family in New Mexico* (New York: Alfred S. Knopf, 1968), 276-277; Ibid., 262-263; Interview, Nellie Ruth Jones, October 16, 2003.

[153] Interview, Nellie Ruth Jones, October 16, 2003; "Removal attempt made in 1925," *Lincoln County News*, May 12, 1961.

[154] Interview, Nellie Ruth Jones, October 16, 2003; "Passing of Frank Coe," *Alamogordo News*, September 24, 1931; Typescript, "Public Meeting," in Blazer Family Papers, Special Collections, University of Arizona Libraries, Box 1, Folder 11; "Interesting Picnic Sponsored by C. of C. Sun. at Mescalero," *Alamogordo News*, June 16, 1932; George W. Coe, *Frontier Fighter-The autobiography of George W. Coe who fought and rode with Billy the Kid, as Related to Nan Hillary Harrison* (Boston, MA: Houghton Mifflin Co., 1934); "George W. Coe funeral Saturday," *Albuquerque Journal*, November 13, 1941.

[155] Helen C. LaMay to William V. Morrison, April 24, 1950, in Eve Ball Papers, 1855-1984, MSS3096, Box 26, Folder 6, Brigham Young University.

[156] "Lincoln County Memorial Commission Plans Restoration of Area's Landmarks, Relics," *El Paso Times*, June 25, 1950; "In New Mexico," *Albuquerque Journal*, August 4, 1950.

[157] "Lincoln County Memorial Commission Plans Restoration," *El Paso Times*, June 25, 1950.

[158] Maurice G. Fulton to Jeff Dykes, October 13, 1950, Jeff Dykes Papers, Cushing Memorial Library and Archives, Texas A&M University Special Collections.

[159] Ibid.

[160] "Historian Resigns," *Albuquerque Journal*, January 11, 1951.

[161] "Legislative Summary," in *Albuquerque Journal*, March 11, 1951; Robert N. Mullin to Col. Maurice Fulton, April 16, 1951, Fulton Papers, Special Collections, University of Arizona Libraries, Box 3, Folder 4; "W.A. Keleher Appointed to Old Lincoln Board," *Albuquerque Journal*, July 13, 1951. Fulton was seeking recovery of a number of items, one of which was one of Charlie Siringo's books. In April, he still quibbled with the Commission over this item.

[162] "Boylans Resign Posts; Did Much for Lincoln," *El Paso Times*, August 11, 1965, in Morgue File, Lincoln, Historical Society for Southeast New Mexico, Roswell, NM; Lincoln County Collection, Courtesy Palace of the Governors Photo Archives (NMHM/DCA) 104886. Photograph and Identification of Old Lincoln County Memorial Commission by James Marshall.

[163] "Drama of Coronado's Trip in Southwest a Three-State Feature," *Albuquerque Journal*, April 30, 1940; "Billy the Kid Drama Planned at Famed Scene," *Albuquerque Journal*, April 30, 1940; Cameron Douglas, "Hello Bob," *True West*, April 28, 2015.

[164] "Billy the Kid Drama Planned," *Albuquerque Journal*, April 30, 1940; "Western Artist Peter Hurd Dies of Alzheimer's," *Hartford Courant*, July 10, 1984; "'Kid' Rides Streets of Old Lincoln Again This Weekend," *Alamogordo Daily News*, August 5, 1955. The "Last Escape of Billy the Kid" remains popular to this day and

is still performed annually. The Kid was portrayed by a number of local citizens after Peter Hurd, including a long run by actor Johnny Thomas.

[165] "Liggett Meigs," *Lubbock Avalanche-Journal*, September 5, 2003; Dr. Jon Hunner, "John Meigs: The Collector's Eye," in *John Meigs: The Collector's Eye* (Las Cruces, NM: University Art Gallery, New Mexico State University, 1997), 7; Mark S. Fuller, *Never a Dull Moment* (Santa Fe: Sunstone Press, 2015), 15; Ibid., 19; Ibid., 22; Ibid., 28-31; Ibid., 33-35.

[166] Fuller, *Never a Dull Moment*, 62-65; Ibid., 78-79; Debora Rindge, "A Vision in San Patricio: The Collection of John Meigs," in Catalog, *John Meigs: The Collector's Eye,* 11.

[167] W.F. Coe to Mr. W.A. Keleher, Albuquerque, N. Mex., May 19, 1960, William A. Keleher Papers, Collection MSS742 BC, Box 14, Folder 1, University of New Mexico, Center for Southwest Research.

[168] "Memorandum of Understanding & Agreement, on Lincoln County Historical Society letterhead, July 12, 1960, in Keleher Papers, Collection MSS742 BC, Box 14, Folder 1, University of New Mexico, Center of Southwest Research; Kate McGaw, "The Faces of Lincoln Town," *New Mexico Magazine,* January 1983, 54.

[169] "Boylans Resign Posts," *El Paso Times,* August 11, 1965; McGaw, "The Faces of Lincoln Town," *New Mexico Magazine,* 56; Matt Bosisio, "La Paloma Museum preserves past," *Roswell Daily Record*, July 28, 1985; Notes, Joe Salazar, Undated, ca. 2013, at his home in Salazar Canyon, Lincoln County, New Mexico. Theodora's father was Refugio Romero (1861-1933), who first ran the dry goods store in Lincoln with his wife Roberta Chavez Romero (1875-1969). Mrs. Maes reported that she unlocked the door for Douglas Fairbanks, who rewarded her with a five-dollar tip.

[170] "Court to Pass on Historic Lincoln Tract," *Albuquerque Journal,* May 10, 1958.

[171] Copy of Letter, Mrs .John Boylan to Mr. Dan Sosa, District Attorney, July 16, 1960, William A. Keleher Papers, Collection MSS742 BC, Box 14, Box 1, University of New Mexico, Center for Southwest Research.

[172] Notes, Joe Salazar, Undated, ca. 2013, Salazar Canyon, Lincoln County, New Mexico; Petition by Lincoln County Residents to Hon. Marshall Milner, July 15, 1960; Mrs. John Boylan to Mr. W.A. Keleher, July 23, 1960, William A. Keleher Papers, University of New Mexico, Center for Southwest Research. Mrs. Boylan still referred to the "La Paloma Bar" in May 1962, although a news article indicates a "former bar" in 1967. The museum lasted until the late 1980s.

[173] Philip J. Rasch, "Clues to The Puzzle of Billy the Kid," in Robert K. DeArment, comp., *Trailing Billy the Kid*, 53. Originally in English Westerner's *Brand Book*, December 1957-January 1958.

[174] Ibid.; W.A.K. [William A. Keleher] to Robert N. Mullin, June 6, 1959, Robert N. Mullin Collection, Haley Memorial Library and History Center, Midland, Texas; Clarence Monroe Burton, William Stocking, and Gordon K. Miller, *The City of Detroit, Michigan, 1701-1922, Volume 3* (Detroit and Chicago, IL: S.J. Clarke Publishing Company, 1922), 897-898.

[175] Burton, ed., *City of Detroit*, V. 3, 897; Lois Telfer, U.S. Social Security Death Index, Master File, New York, Social Security Administration, Record Group 47, National Archives & Records Administration; "Mrs. Telfer Files Maintenance Suit," *Detroit Free Press,* July 24, 1936.

[176] Enid V. Rosenblum to Author, undated but envelope postmarked May 15, 2015. Lois' letters always referred to Vigilante, who she knew from the history library in New York, as "Vig." He was a respected librarian there for many years, who co-wrote some of the "You Were There" books about the American West.

[177] Ibid.

[178] W.A.K. to Mullin, June 6, 1959, Mullin Collection, Haley Memorial Library and History Center, Midland, Texas.

[179] Lois Telfer to Robert N. Mullin, August 2, [1959], Robert N. Mullin Collection, Haley Memorial Library and History Center, Midland, Texas. On the reverse of the letter, in Telfer's handwriting, is several notes about people to see in New Mexico. The names included Omar Barker, Ward Leslie, and Fred Lambert.

[180] Philip J. Rasch to Lois Telfer, August 14, 1959, Robert N. Mullin Collection, Haley Memorial Library and History Center, Midland, Texas. The *Lincoln County News* announced her visit a week after she departed. It was mentioned as a "short visit" and she met with H.A. Huey in Capitan and Ward Leslie in Carrizozo.

[181] "He had Friends and was not Evil, Says Kid's Red-Haired 'Cousin,'" *Albuquerque Journal*, May 13, 1960.

[182] Interview, Nellie Ruth Jones, October 16, 2013.

[183] Ibid.

[184] "Lincoln War, 80 Years Old Still Rouses Hard Feelings," *Las Cruces Sun-News,* July 3, 1960. The same basic article also ran in the *Clovis News-Journal* (July 10, 1960) and the *Las Vegas (NM) Daily Optic,* June 23, 1960.

[185] "Fate of famed Lincoln Pageant hangs in balance," *Lincoln County News*, December 9, 1960.

[186] Lincoln County Commissioner's Record, Volume 5, 509; "Move made to re-inter 'The Kid' in Lincoln County," *Lincoln County News*, April 14, 1961. Baker, an active member of the interested citizen's group, penned an editorial called "Let's settle this matter for all time," in the same issue.

[187] This word-for-word version was taken directly from the De Baca County Commissioner's Journal, Volume 2, 423. Note there are differences in the edited version published in the April 14, 1961 issue of the *Lincoln County News*. It is uncertain if errors were made in the original letter or in transcription.

[188] De Baca County Commissioner's Journal, Volume 2, 423.

[189] There seemed to be inevitability about the matter among Lincoln residents. Perhaps they felt Fort Sumner officials would agree to terms.

[190] Paul Baker, "Let's settle this matter for all time," *Lincoln County News*, April 14, 1961.

[191] Ibid.

[192] Ibid.

[193] Entry of May 4, 1961, Lincoln County Commissioners Record, Volume 5, 509; Entry of May 4, 1961, Commissioner's Meeting, De Baca County Commissioner's Journal, Volume 2, 424-425.

[194] Letter to Board [De Baca] County Commissioners, May 8, 1961, Lincoln County Commissioners Record, Volume 5, 516.

[195] Interview, Sharon Degner, Alamogordo, NM, July 18, 2013. Mrs. Degner was the second wife of Joe O. Sargent and a witness during this time.

[196] Joe Sargent, Texas Department of State Health Services, Texas Birth Index, 1903-1997; 1930 United States Federal Census, Hale County, Texas, T626, Roll 2339, NARA; Interview, Sharon Degner, Alamogordo, NM, July 18, 2013.

[197] Interview, Sharon Degner, Alamogordo, NM, July 18, 2013; Johnson S. Stearns, *Small Town Magic* (White Oaks, NM: Birdsong's Press, 1997), 2-3; Johnson Stearns and Ann Buffington, *Looking Back-A Photo History of Carrizozo* (Carrizozo, NM: Lincoln County Historical Society, ca. 1999), Introduction; Additional Information was gained from a personal visit to Mr. Stearns in Carrizozo, NM on October 20, 2013. He passed away on October 10, 2015.

[198] Interview, Eugene and Sharon Degner, Alamogordo, NM, July 18, 2013; Alan Rhodes, Ancestry.com, *Social Security Death Index* [database on-line] Provo, UT, USA: Ancestry.com Operations Inc, 2011. Original data: Social Security Administration, *Social Security Death Index, Master File.* Social Security Administration; L.H.T. [Lois Telfer] to R.N.M. [Robert N. Mullin], August 16 [1961], Robert N. Mullin Collection, Haley Memorial Library and History Center, Midland, Texas. Telfer admitted to Mullin, "I hate publicity, but at the urging of Alan Rhodes, (son of Eugene Manlove Rhodes) & Helena Coe LaMay....I offered to help..."

[199] "Relative of Wm. Bonney supports move to re-inter remains of "The Kid" in Lincoln County Park," *Lincoln County News*, April 28, 1961. Lloyd Leslie Davis, Jr. (1931-2016), a Texan who graduated from New Mexico Military Institute in 1955. After a stint in the Army, Davis settled permanently in Ruidoso, where he served three times as mayor. He was interviewed by the author.

[200] Ibid.

[201] Ibid.

[202] Ibid.

[203] Ibid.

[204] Ibid.; William V. Morrison to Paul Baker, May 14, 1961, Sonnichsen Collection, MS141, Box 118, Folder 839, University of Texas at El Paso Library, Special Collections Department.

[205] Morrison to Baker, May 14, 1961, Sonnichsen Collection, MS141, Box 118, Folder 839, University of Texas at El Paso Library, Special Collections Department.

[206] Ibid.

[207] Ibid.

[208] Ibid.

[209] Interview, Sharon Degner, Alamogordo, NM, July 18, 2013. The author contacted the current owner of the Meigs mural from the Yucca Bar, but never viewed it personally to be able to include a full description. There is also no mention in Mark S. Fuller's comprehensive biography on Meigs, but this was a prolific period for the artist.

[210] Ibid.; Copy, Notes of Historian Donald Lavash, Undated. Sometimes just known as "Escape of Billy the Kid," Lavash used the famous painting for the inside boards of a history book on New Mexico.

[211] L.H.T. [Telfer] to R.N.M. [Mullen], August 16, [1961], Mullin Collection, Haley Memorial Library and History Center, Midland, Texas; William V. Morrison to Paul Baker, May 14, 1961, Sonnichsen Collection, MS141, Box 118, Folder 839, University of Texas at El Paso Library, Special Collections. Morrison suggested "Mr. [Wilbur] Coe, Mr. [George] Penfield, Ernest Key, or someone else capable of researching their legal records in a most thorough manner." Marguerite or Margaret Salazar (1901-1997) was the adopted daughter of Yginio (1863-1936), and was well-versed on the Kid through her father.

[212] Interview, Nellie Ruth Jones, Glencoe, NM, October 16, 2013; "Fate of Billy's body up to courts now as attorney files petition," *Lincoln County News*, June 9, 1961; U.S. Army Enlistment Record, World War II, Record Group 64, National Archives and Records Administration; "Clarence C. Chase Will Run For Office of District Judge On Republican Ticket Here," *Las Cruces Sun-News,* March 4, 1956. Nellie Ruth Jones noted that Fall was not popular for defending powerful rancher Oliver Lee, who was strongly suspected of the deaths of Colonel A.J. Fountain and his son in 1896.

[213] Invitation, Wortley Hotel Luncheon for May 30, 1961, Sonnichsen Collection, MS 141, Box 136, Folder 1074, University of Texas at El Paso Library, Special Collections. A second invitation was found at the University of Texas, Briscoe Center.

[214] Ibid.

[215] "Arrives," *El Paso Times*, May 27, 1961; "Western Welcome Set for Kin of Billy the Kid," *El Paso Herald-Post*, May 25, 1961; Marshall Hail, "Billy the Kid's Only Surviving Relative Isn't Talking Here," *El Paso Herald- Post*, May 26, 1961.

[216] "Lincoln Countians invited to De Baca County to learn all about its "glorious history," *Lincoln County News*, May 26, 1961. Only the first and final paragraphs are not quoted here.

[217] Paul Baker, "De Baca County, in defensive move, attacks pageant given by Lincoln County," *Lincoln County News*, May 26, 1961. The remaining two paragraphs go into the details of the pageant and memorial park.

[218] L.H.T. to R.N.M., August 16 [1961], Mullin Collection, Haley Library and History Center, Midland, TX; Obituary, Pauline Garrett, *Albuquerque Journal*, March 9, 1981. Pauline was 80 years of age when she passed. Of all Pat Garrett's children, only her brother Jarvis survived her. She was known to avoid being

photographed and was humble. In one interview for the *Las Cruces Sun-News* (November 22, 1970), Pauline stated, "I did nothing but stay here."

[219] L.H.T. to R.N.M., August 16 [1961], Mullin Collection, Haley Library; 1940 Census, Mesilla, Dona Ana County, New Mexico, T627, Roll 2443, Page 8A, National Archives and Records Administration; Bill McGaw, "Lincoln County People Unite to Obtain Possession of Billy the Kid's Bones," *El Paso Herald-Post*, May 30, 1961. Elizabeth (1897-1977) and her family founded the Gadsden Museum, which exists today.

[220] Bill McGaw, "Lincoln County People Unite to Obtain Possession of Billy the Kid's Bones," El Paso Herald-Post, May 30, 1961.

[221] Ibid.

[222] Ibid.; Notes from Interview, Joe Salazar, Undated; "Mrs. Maes Recalls Father's Exploits in 'Lincoln War," *Alamogordo Daily News*, April 10, 1957; "Nearly 85, She Recalls Events of Lincoln War," *Alamogordo Daily News,* January 30, 1966. Alan Rhodes related that his father Eugene thought George Coe's book to be the most authentic about the Lincoln County War.

[223] McGaw, "Lincoln County People Unite to Obtain Possession of Billy the Kid's Bones," *El Paso Herald-Post*, May 30, 1961.

[224] [William V. Morrison], "Efforts recalled to locate judgment in death of 'Kid," *Lincoln County News*, June 2, 1961; D. Vernon Payne, "A Ballad of Lonely Bill," in "Writer Sends Yet Another New Ballad of Billy the Kid," *Lincoln County News*, June 2, 1961; "Excitement grows over Billy's Body," *Lincoln County News,* June 2, 1961. Sheriff Bradley apparently said so in jest.

[225] The territorial press during Billy the Kid's time was often utilized for partisan or controlled purposes. Ash Upson was editor of a newspaper before he served as ghostwriter for Pat Garrett's book. The "House" also controlled some of their message through the press. See Porter A. Stratton, *The Territorial Press of New Mexico 1834-1912* (Albuquerque, NM. University of New Mexico Press, 1969).

[226] Debs Smith, "The Battle for Billy's Bones, "*Impact-Albuquerque Journal Magazine,* April 7, 1961, 6; Burton, *The City of Detroit Vol. 3*, 897; R.N. Mullin to Lois Telfer, June 9, 1959, Keleher Papers, University of New Mexico, Center for Southwest Research; "Western Welcome Set for Kin of Billy the Kid," *El Paso Herald-Post,* May 25, 1961; "He Had Friends and Was Not Evil, Says Kid's Red-Haired 'Cousin," *Albuquerque Journal,* May 13, 1960. Lois Telfer, as explained later, was not the "last surviving relative," as there were other cousins and her brother, still alive.

[227] "He Had Friends and Was Not Evil, Says Kid's Red-Haired'Cousin,"*Albuquerque Journal,* May 13, 1960; Smith, "Battle for Billy's Bones," *Impact*, April 7, 1961, 6. At least one billboard still existed during the author's visit to Fort Sumner.

[228] Philip J. Rasch to C.L. Sonnichsen, June 5, 1961, Sonnichsen Collection, MS141, Box 138, Folder 1101, University of Texas at El Paso Library, Special Collections.

[229] Ibid; Grady E. McCright, "Who Sleeps in Billy the Kid's Tomb?," *True Frontier,* April 1978, 47; Maurice Fulton [from Jack Potter], "The Grave of the Kid and its

Marker," University of Texas at Austin, Dolph Briscoe Center for American History.

230 Map, Chas. W. Burrow, in Fort Sumner File, Record Group 393, Records of United States Army Commands, 1821-1920, National Archives and Records Administration. During a visit to the now-defunct Old Fort Museum, the author was told the back grave was probably O'Folliard.

231 Ibid.; James N. Warner to Mrs. R.A. Doak, April 6, 1940, History Colorado Center (formerly Colorado Historical Society), Denver, Colorado; McCright, "Who Sleeps in Billy the Kid's Tomb?," *True Frontier,* April 1978, 12-13. The Old Fort Museum, which is at the burial site, had a docent who revealed the account of the sidewalk. In addition, there was a headstone made for the Kid, which was later stolen.

232 "Fate of Billy's body up to courts now as attorney files petition," *Lincoln County News and Carrizozo Outlook*, June 9, 1961.

233 Ibid.

234 Bob [Robert N. Mullin] to Leland Sonnichsen, June 23, 1961, in Sonnichsen Collection, MS141, Box 136, Folder 1074, University of Texas at El Paso Library, Special Collections.

235 Ibid.

236 Petition No. 3255, District Court of the Tenth Judicial District Within and For the County of De Baca, De Baca County Clerk's Office; Civil Docket, No. 3255, De Baca County Clerk's Office; Summons, Board of Commissioners of De Baca County and Mrs. J.W. Allen, in No. 3255, De Baca County Clerk's Office.

237 Petition, Case No. 3255, District Court of the Tenth Judicial District Within and For the County of De Baca [New Mexico].

238 "Outlaw's Grave Feud Rages," *El Paso Herald-Post,* June 27, 1961.

239 "Guns' Might Start Firing Again Though Billy the Kid is Gone," *El Paso Herald-Post,* June 30, 1961.

240 Ibid. The "irate relatives" were the Maxwell Family. There had been a number of complaints about the cemetery publicly aired by a descendant.

241 Ibid.

242 Hoyt Gimlin, "Two New Mexico Towns Fight for the Remains of Billy the Kid," *Milwaukee Journal Green Sheet*, June 30, 1961.

243 "Pageant plans set," *Lincoln County News*, July 7, 1961. Nan Boylan would make this clear in letters later in the year.

244 "Moving the Kid's Bones Hits Snag," *Arizona Republic*, July 5, 1961.

245 Editorial, "Lincoln County "cruel" says De Baca county newspaper editorial, reprinted in *Lincoln County News*, July 13, 1961, from original in *De Baca County News.*

246 Motion to Dismiss Petition, in Petition of Removal of William H. Bonney, Deceased, to Board of County Commissioners and Mrs. J.W. Allen, No. 3255, De Baca County Courthouse; Phone Interview, Myrl Jane Humphrey, October 7, 2013.

[247] "Charlie Bowdre's relative wants no digging," *Lincoln County News*, July 20, 1961. The letter was written on July 5, the same day as the *World*'s article.

[248] Obituary, Louis Allen Bowdre, *[Bartlesville, OK] Examiner-Enterprise*, December 31, 2004; Interview Notes, Sue Tennell, Bartlesville, Oklahoma, September 9, 2013.

[249] Motion to Dismiss Petition, No. 3255, John Humphrey, Jr., Assistant District Attorney, Tenth Judicial District, July 18, 1961; Phone Interview, Myrl Jane Humphrey, October 7, 2013.

[250] "New judge sought for Kid hearing," *Lincoln County News*, July 27, 1961; Affidavit of Disqualification, Case No. 3255; Order Designating Judge, Case No. 3255.

[251] "New judge named," *Lincoln County News*, August 3, 1961; "Move for decent burial," *Lincoln County News*, August 3, 1961.

[252] "Move for decent burial," *Lincoln County News*, August 3, 1961.

[253] L.H.T. for W.H.B. [Lois Telfer] to R.N.M [Robert N. Mullin], August 16, [1961], in Robert N. Mullin Collection, Haley Memorial Library and History Center, Midland, Texas.

[254] Ibid.

[255] Ibid.

[256] Keleher was not known as a Telfer admirer, and gave her little notice in his writings. This was probably due to his opposition to the Brushy Bill Roberts controversy In 1950, and influence from other doubting forces, such as the Boylans in Lincoln. It is curious that he and Telfer exchanged letters at this time.

[257] Interview, Sharon Degner, Alamogordo, New Mexico, July 18, 2013.

[258] "Tragedy strikes Sargents as house blown to bits," *Lincoln County News*, August 24, 1961; "Services held here for Joe Sargent," *Lincoln County News*, August 31, 1961; Interview, Sharon Degner, Alamogordo, New Mexico, July 18, 2013.

[259] "Services held here for Joe Sargent," *Lincoln County News*, August 31, 1961; Interview, Sharon Degner, Alamogordo, New Mexico, July 18, 2013.

[260] Ibid.

[261] L.H.T. to R.N.M., October 23 [1961], in Robert N. Mullin Collection, Haley Memorial Library and History Center, Midland, Texas.

[262] Ibid.

[263] Helena C. LaMay to William V. Morrison, October 10, 1961, Eve Ball Papers, MS 3096, Box 26, Folder 6, L. Tom Perry Special Collections, Brigham Young University.

[264] Obituary, "Louis A. Bowdre Sr.," *Bartlesville Examiner-Enterprise*, December 30, 2004; Information from Sue Tennell, Bartlesville, Oklahoma, September 9, 2013. After Louis Bowdre's initial reaction in the summer of 1961, there was little thought of an in-depth interview. It was surprising that contemporaries, particularly Telfer, failed to mention Louis Bowdre in their existing letters.

[265] Information from Betty Grabbe and Phil Scott; Emails, Betty Grabbe to Author, July 9 and July 13, 2012; Personal Visit, Tombstone of Benjamin Thomas Bowdre Family, Plumerville Cemetery, Plumerville, Arkansas. The author's research into Charlie Bowdre's family found direct descendants from most of his siblings, including his favorite brother Benjamin (who had three living children: Paul Hull Bowdre, Esther Bowdre Newbern, and Elizabeth Bowdre Allison—Betty Grabbe's mother) and Eppie Bowdre Dockery, who married Donald McKay Dockery (four children living in 1962: Ramelle Morgan, Eppie Forsythe, Albert Dockery, Donald Dockery, Jr.). The Dockery Family resided in Hernando, Mississippi for generations.

[266] Eastwood, ed., *Nuestras Madres*, 92-93. Miguel Antonio Otero, after his service as New Mexico's governor, wrote *The Real Billy the Kid*. The book was published in 1936 by Rufus Rockwell Wilson of New York. Prior to this, he penned *My Life on the Frontier 1864-1882,* published by Press of the Pioneers, New Haven, Connecticut. A third volume of memoirs of his years as governor (1897-1906) was published later. Otero died in 1944. The Works Progress Administration (WPA) interviewed numerous Spanish allies of Billy the Kid during the mid-1930s, including members of the Chavez and Trujillo families.

[267] Information from Myrl Jane Humphrey, October 7, 2013. In the process of interviewing Humphrey's daughter by phone, it was learned her father, the Assistant District Attorney, was a student of local history. This energized his zealous representation. There was little belief that Humphrey knew more than basic knowledge of Bowdre's family and was willing to rely on Louis Bowdre. In fact, Sue Tennell (Louis Bowdre's daughter) felt Humphrey knew of Charlie, but primarily through her father.

[268] "Billy the Kid back in the news, court hearing set for Nov. 16," *Lincoln County News*, November 9, 1961; "First Appeals Chief Judge Die in SF [Santa Fe] This Morning," *Santa Fe New Mexican*, November 22, 1967.

[269] "Judge Will Hear Petition to Move Body of 'Kid,' *Albuquerque Journal*, November 17, 1961. Floods, such as the one in 1904, contributed to some vanished markers. However, as explained, the Kid's marker was gone before this.

[270] Ibid.

[271] Ibid.

[272] Ibid.

[273] "Answer to Petition," in Case No. 3255, District Court of the Tenth Judicial District Within and for the County of De Baca, Filed November 22, 1961.

[274] Ibid.

[275] Ibid.

[276] Lois Telfer to R.N.M. [Mullin], Nov. 29 [1961], Robert N. Mullin Collection, Haley Memorial Library and History Center, Midland, Texas. She wrote about threats connected with the case and referred to their connection with the death of Sargent. There has never been proof of foul play, but the timing of the

circumstance propelled questions. Telfer had just sent Sargent a power of attorney that week.

[277] Ibid. Most of the letter was on the topic of the Bonney surname and not the hearing. Mullin wanted to know about the name "Henry McCarty" and its association with the Kid. Telfer claimed a Grant County newspaper reported this name as the Kid confused two different individuals. Further, he picked up the alias while in hiding. This must have raised the eyebrows of Mullin, who was a "stickler" for research.

[278] Mrs. John Boylan to Mr. W.A. Keleher, December 1, 1961, William A. Keleher Papers, Collection MSS742 BC, University of New Mexico, Center for Southwest Studies, Box 14, Folder 2.

[279] Ibid.

[280] Ibid.

[281] Ibid.; "Billy the Kid Will Ride Again in Lincoln Pageant," Albuquerque Journal, July 30, 1961. The latter and identification of a related photograph identified the full names of the other commission members. Nan Boylan's complaints with Ramon Maes surfaced in this letter, linking her preservation battles with that of the Telfer case.

[282] Boylan to Keleher, December 1, 1961, Keleher Papers, University of New Mexico, Center for Southwest Studies, Collection MSS742 BC, Box 14, Folder 2.

[283] Copy of Letter, William A. Keleher to the Boylans, December 4, 1961, William A. Keleher Papers, University of New Mexico, Center for Southwest Studies.

[284] Ibid.

[285] "Billy's Future is Looking Brighter," Lincoln County News, November 23, 1961.

[286] Bill Fritch, as reported in "Billy's Future is Looking Brighter," Lincoln County News, November 23, 1961.

[287] "Motion to Intervene," in Case No. 3255, District Court of the Tenth Judicial District Within and for the County of De Baca, filed December 6, 1961.

[288] "Final Order," Case 2184, District Court of De Baca County, New Mexico, Manuel Abreu, F.W. Spitz, Kenneth Miller, Frank Lavato, Juanita Gonzales, Mrs. Mike Williams, Mrs. J.O. Welborn, and Celistino Sandoval Vs. John W. Allen, "Exhibit A," Case No. 3255, District Court of the Tenth Judicial District Within and for the County of De Baca. John W. Allen died in 1945, survived by his wife and three children.

[289] Humphrey used the older case to prove the cemetery was of value to the community and that Mrs. Allen was not party to the petition. With Louis Bowdre's Petition to Intervene, it proved the best strategy.

[290] The author conducted a study of Louis A. Bowdre's family connection to Charlie Bowdre, due to the emphasis in 1961-62 news reports. There is no mention of the claim in Louis Bowdre's obituary or in later articles. After going back six generations of this family, their roots are in Ohio. Charlie Bowdre's family stayed in the South, with Georgia and Mississippi the root areas. At no time during these six generations did these family lines cross. It is possible that

there was an earlier connection, but any claim of close kinship in 1961 would be difficult to prove. Interviews of family members in Arkansas and Mississippi do not recall this family. Therefore, the official claim of the court could not have withstood scrutiny.

[291] Information from Sue Tennell, Bartlesville, Oklahoma, September 9, 2013; "Our Representative W.H. Bowdre," *Watonga Herald*, September 26, 1907.

[292] "Our Representative W.H. Bowdre," *Watonga Herald*, September 26, 1907. Census records show Judge Bowdre was born in Ohio, and G.W. Bowdre, Louis A.'s father, was a Missouri native.

[293] "Oklahoma relative of Charlie Bowdre enters the court case of Billy the Kid," *Lincoln County News,* December 14, 1961.

[294] Lois H. Telfer to Phil Cooke, December 6 [1961], 1972-002 Philip St. George Cooke III Collection, State Archives of New Mexico, Santa Fe, New Mexico.

[295] Ibid.

[296] Bill Kelly, "Bowdre mystery yet to be laid to rest," *New Mexico Magazine*, February 1993, 34; "Arizona woman claims to be third cousin of Billy, indicates many other relatives," *Lincoln County News*, December 7, 1961. Neither claim carried much further weight in the hearings, except a ruling that further petitions was shut off by Judge Hensley in January.

[297] "Another Round in Billy the Kid Fuss Scheduled," *Albuquerque Journal*, January 9, 1962; Information from Sue Tennell, September 9, 2013.

[298] Lois H. Telfer to Phil Cooke, January 17, 1962, 1972-002 Philip St. George Cooke III Collection, State Archives of New Mexico, Santa Fe, New Mexico. The notation at bottom of page, likely Cooke, wrote the date "1887" was a typo, and it should have stated "1877."

[299] Response to Motion to Intervene, Case No. 3255, District Court of De Baca County, New Mexico, January 11, 1962.

[300] "Oklahoman gets intervenor rights!" *Lincoln County News*, January 25, 1962.

[301] Answer to Petition, Case No. 3255, District Court of the Tenth Judicial District Within and for the County of De Baca, Filed January 24, 1962.

[302] After the author interviewed a number of relatives in Arkansas and Mississippi, it became apparent that the family was unaware of the Telfer case. Despite the publicity, several descendants knew well that Charlie died in New Mexico Territory yet little else. However, there might have been another reason for their silence. Betty Grabbe, the granddaughter of Charlie's brother, stated the family were not to discuss Charlie. Her Aunt Esther Newbern related "forbidden" details of Charlie's friendship with the Kid. Even in 1962, many families still distanced themselves from outlaw kin. Hence, some may have read about the case, but hesitated involvement. Even so, these Arkansas and Mississippi relatives do not remember any contact from Humphrey.

[303] "Oklahoman gets intervenor rights!" *Lincoln County News*, January 25, 1962.

[304] Clarissa Fuller, "Large Safety Pins in Kid's Grave Could be Important," *Albuquerque Tribune*, January 27, 1962.

[305] Chester Chope, "This Fabulous Southwest," *El Paso Herald-Post*, February 6, 1962.

[306] John Humphrey, Jr. to Wm. V. Morrison, January 30, 1962, Sonnichsen Collection, MS141, University of Texas at El Paso Library, Special Collections, Box 118, Folder 839. Morrison's 1950 introduction of Brushy Bill left a "chip on his shoulder," and his primary interest was proving his point. Although at the May 1961 luncheon at the Wortley Hotel with the "Friends," he was not necessarily a staunch ally.

[307] Ibid.

[308] Wm. V. Morrison to John Humphrey, Jr., February 8, 1962, Sonnichsen Collection, MS141, University of Texas at El Paso Library, Special Collections, Box 118, Folder 839. Flattered at being asked, Morrison's letter was primarily about the lack of evidence of a burial.

[309] Ibid.

[310] Ibid.

[311] John Humphrey to R.N. Mullin, February 14, 1962, Robert N. Mullin Collection, Haley Memorial Library and History Center, Midland, TX. The author did not find a copy of the February 6 letter.

[312] S [Sylvester] Vigilante to Philip St. George Cooke III, February 17, 1962, 1972-002 Philip St. George Cooke III Collection, State Archives of New Mexico. Note the question mark about Telfer being the only relative, which insinuates Vigilante was not sure himself. That probably raised questions in Cooke's mind.

[313] George Dixon, "Billy the Kid Still Famous," *Fairbanks [AK] Daily News-Miner*, February 2, 1962.

[314] Dudley M. Lynch, "They're Still Arguing about Billy (The Kid) Bonney," *Alamogordo Daily News*, February 21, 1962.

[315] John McMillion, "Trial Could Answer Questions: Who Was Billy the Kid? Was He Really Killed?" *El Paso Herald-Post*, March 3, 1962.

[316] Copy, Witness Card and Subpoena in Case No. 3255, Filed March 6, 1962, Tenth Judicial District, County of De Baca; Lincoln County Board of Commissioners, Typed Notes, March 5, 1962, 15. The full notation read: "Clerk was instructed to write to Mr. C C Chase, Attorney at law, also to Lloyd Davis Jr and the Chamber of Commerce at Ruidoso in regards to the removal of the remains of William Bonney, alias "Billy the Kid" from De Baca County to Lincoln County, Interment to be in Lincoln, first County Seat in Lincoln County. There are no funds available in the county at this time and it would be impossible to get approval for a fund because of two counties involved."

[317] "Services Friday For Mrs. Hensley," *Amarillo Globe*, March 8, 1962; "Sophronia Ellen Hensley," Find-A-Grave, database and images (http://www.findagrave.com), memorial page for Sophronia Ellen Hensley (3 Oct 1873-7 Mar 1962), Find A Grave Memorial no. 13224996, citing Portales Cemetery, Portales, Roosevelt County, New Mexico, USA; Maintained by Joyce Gore Locke (contributor 46616313); John Humphrey, Jr. to William V. Morrison,

March 14, 1962, Sonnichsen Collection, MS141, University of Texas at El Paso Library, Special Collections, Box 118, Folder 839.

[318] John McMillion, "Trial Opens to Determine Whether Bones of Billy the Kid to Be Moved," *Austin American-Statesman,* March 13, 1962; "Witness and Mural," *Lubbock Avalanche-Journal*, March 14, 1962. There was a picture and caption of Louis Bowdre and the Hunter mural.

[319] John McMillion, "Bones of Billy the Kid to Stay at Fort Sumner," *Longview News-Journal*, March 15, 1962; John Humphrey, Jr. to William V. Morrison, March 14, 1962, Sonnichsen Collection, MS141, University of Texas at El Paso Library, Special Collections, Box 118, Folder 839.

[320] L.H.T.[Telfer] to R.N.M.[Mullin], May 22 [1962], Robert N. Mullin Collection, Haley Memorial Library, Midland, Texas.

[321] Information from Sue Tennell; "Billy the Kid's Bones Stay in New Mexico," *The Monitor [McAllen, TX]*, March 14, 1962; "Billy's Bones to Stay Put; Dismissal Motion Upheld," *El Paso Herald-Post*, March 13, 1962; McMillion, "Bones of Billy," *Longview News-Journal*, March 15, 1962.

[322] Kenneth May, "Kid' To Remain In Fort Sumner Grave," *Lubbock Avalanche-Journal,* March 14, 1962.

[323] A comparison of family records confirms the disparity. This does not mean that Louis Bowdre did not believe it to be true—indeed he may have. After the author's discussion with his daughter Sue, Louis certainly believed in his cause and may have grown up believing an incorrect relationship. All I can confirm that the reported relationship in both the final court filing (as the nearest kin) and the *Lubbock Avalanche-Journal* is not true, regardless of the reason.

[324] "Billy the Kid's Bones Stay," *The Monitor*, March 14, 1962.

[325] May, "Kid' To Remain in Fort Sumner Grave, *Lubbock Avalache-Journal*, March 14, 1962.

[326] "Billy the Kid's Bones Stay," *The Monitor,* March 14, 1962.

[327] "Witness and Mural," *Lubbock Avalanche-Journal*, March 14, 1962; "At Billy's Grave," *Alamogordo Daily News,* March 20, 1962.

[328] Humphrey, Jr. to Morrison, March 14, 1962, Sonnichsen Collection, MS141, University of Texas at El Paso Library, Special Collections, Box 118, Folder 839.

[329] Copy, William Morrison to John Humphrey, Jr., March 15, 1962, Sonnichsen Collection, University of Texas at El Paso Library, Special Collections, Box 118, Folder 839.

[330] Ibid.

[331] Ibid.

[332] "Billy's bones rest in peace," *Lincoln County News*, March 15, 1962.

[333] Ibid.

[334] "At Billy's Grave," *Alamogordo Daily News*, March 20, 1962.

[335] Postcard of Billy the Kid mailed by "Cecil" to Jeff Dykes, postmarked from Fort Sumner, March 1962, Author's Collections. "Cecil" was likely Cecil Bonney, a Pecos Valley resident and author himself who only shared the surname of the

Kid. Dykes worked for the U.S.D.A. Soil Conservation Service at the time and was involved in the Potomac Westerners.

[336] Aside from local histories and a few mentions in wider glances, the Telfer case is largely overlooked. Past historians generally did this for several reasons. Most of the last generation of historians lived through this and are too close to the sources. Enough time has now passed. Secondly, the modern case was more a passing interest.

[337] Notice, Case No. 3255, In Re Application of Lois Telfer, March 30, 1962; Decree, In Re Application of Lois Telfer, April 6, 1962.

[338] Decree, Case No. 3255, In Re Application of Lois Telfer, April 6, 1962.

[339] "Publisher, author raise doubt about final resting spot of Billy the Kid," *Lincoln County News*, April 12, 1962.

[340] L.H.T.[Telfer] to R.N.M.[Mullin], May 22 [1962], Robert N. Mullin Collection, Haley Memorial Library, Midland, Texas.

[341] Ibid.

[342] L. Telfer to R.N.M., September 5 [1965], Robert N. Mullin Collection, Haley Memorial Library and History Center, Midland, TX; Letter to Editor, William J. Carson, ca. January 1966, *Lincoln County News*. The clipping was found in the "Lincoln County Morgue File," Historical Society for Southeast New Mexico, Roswell, New Mexico.

[343] Philip J. Rasch, "Old Problems, New Answers," in *New Mexico Historical Review*, as reproduced in DeArment, ed., *Trailing Billy the Kid*, 116-117.

[344] L. Telfer to R.N.M., September 5 [1965], Robert N. Mullin Collection, Haley Library and History Center, Midland, Texas.

[345] Letter to Editor, William J. Carson, ca. February 1966, *Lincoln County News*. This Clipping was found in the "Lincoln County Morgue File, Historical Society for Southeast New Mexico.

[346] "Alan Rhodes feels he must tell the truth about one William Bonney," *Lincoln County News*, February 24, 1966.

[347] Ibid.

[348] Ibid.

[349] Ibid.

[350] "Morrison willing to carry on fued [sic]," *Lincoln County News*, March 3, 1966.

[351] Ibid.

[352] Ibid.

[353] Ibid.

[354] "Latest developments about 'Bonney was alias," *Lincoln County News*, June 2, 1966.

[355] Ibid. Carson's conclusion about the reasoning behind the dismissal, and most importantly, Telfer's relationship, was not proven or disproven by Judge Hensley's decision.

[356] Ibid.

357 William V. Morrison to Lawrence K. Mooney, April 12, 1977, Sonnichsen Papers, University of Texas at El Paso, Special Collections Department, Box 136, Folder 1073.

358 "W.J. Olds sells interest to Payton," *Lincoln County News*, January 18. 1962; "Taos News Has New Editor; Jim Colegrove to Santa Fe" *Taos News*, November 1, 1962; *Taos News*, November 29, 1962. Payton later bought out his partner.

359 Edward Penfield to William Keleher, December 18, 1965, Keleher Papers, University of New Mexico, Center for Southwest Research, Box 14, Folder 2. Penfield, who relatively new to the Commission himself, attempted to deal with the simmering feud between the Boylans and a number of local citizens, including Roman Maes, Pfingsten and later Walter Henn.

360 Ibid.; "Boylans Resign Posts; Did Much for Lincoln," in Morgue File, Historical Society for Southeast New Mexico.

361 Penfield to Keleher, December 18, 1965, Keleher Papers, University of New Mexico, Center for Southwest Research, Box 14, Folder 2.

362 Ibid.; Klasner [Ball, ed.], *My Girlhood Among Outlaws*, "About the Author and the Editor..."; Mullin, ed., *Fulton's History of the Lincoln County War*, copyright page. Mullin released Fulton's history in 1968, Ball released Klasner's memoir in 1972. Of note was British historian Frederick Nolan's *Life and Death of John Henry Tunstall* in 1965.

363 "Paul Blazer, Sr. Succumbs, 75," *Alamogordo Daily News*, February 28, 1966; Interview, Nellie Ruth Jones, October 16, 2013; "C.C. Chase Rites Today in Alamo," *El Paso Times*, January 9, 1970; "Former District Attorney C.C. Chase, 46 Succumbs," *Las Cruces Sun-News*, January 8, 1970; "Sylvester Vigilante, Summer Vermonter, History Expert, Dies," *Burlington [VT] Free Press,* September 4, 1970; "Alan Rhodes, 69, Dies; Western Novelist's Son," [Binghamton, NY] *Press and Sun-Bulletin,* June 26, 1970.

364 "First Appeals Chief Judge Dies in SF [Santa Fe] This Morning," *Santa Fe New Mexican*, November 22, 1967; "Office Dedicated in Honor of Slain D.A.," *Quay County Sun*, January 12, 2016. The author met and spoke with District Attorney Breen's daughter Viki in Albuquerque.

365 Phil Rasch, "Old Problem, New Answers," in DeArment,ed., *Trailing Billy the Kid*, 116-117; Both Lois and her younger brother, Richard Telfer, lived until his death in June 1980. At no time was his name mentioned at the hearing. Richard Telfer resided in Michigan and had no children.

366 Warner to Doak, April 6, 1940, MS 3079, History Colorado Center (formerly Colorado Historical Society); "Billy the Kid's Stolen Tombstone is Returned," *Daily Herald [Provo, UT]*, May 23, 1976; "Billy the Kid's Tombstone in Possession of Granbury Man," *Hood County [TX] News*, May 13, 1976.

367 "Fort Sumner Park to be Dedicated Today," *Albuquerque Journal*, June 30, 1973; "Dignitaries Help Dedicate Museum at Fort Sumner," *Clovis News-Journal,* July 1, 1973. Mrs. Helene Allen died in Carlsbad, New Mexico on July 22, 1978. John Watson Allen, her late husband, had died in Lubbock, Texas in May 1945.

She is buried in Fort Sumner. The city leased Joe Bowlin the site for his museum for the maximum of 99 years.

[368] Patrick Lamb, "Historic Lincoln Land Wanted," *Santa Fe New Mexican,* October 14, 1976; Richard Benke, "Anderson, Oil Still Mix Well After 50 Years," *Albuquerque Journal,* May 21, 1989; "Interviewing Robert O. Anderson Akin to Jumping a Fast Train," *Albuquerque Journal,* February 8, 1965; "Historic preservation group formed in Lincoln County," *Las Vegas Optic,* April 7, 1977. See Fuller, *Never a Dull Moment.*

[369] "Historic preservation group formed in Lincoln County," *Las Vegas Optic,* April 7, 1977; Fuller, *Never a Dull Moment,* 220-221.

[370] "Historic preservation group formed," *Las Vegas Optic,* April 7, 1977; Fuller, *Never a Dull Moment,* 220-221.

[371] "State museum takes over," *Roswell Daily Record,* June 10, 1979.

[372] William Morrison to G.B. Morrison, December 1, 1975, Copy in Eve Ball Papers, MS 3096, Box 26, Folder 6, Brigham Young University, L. Tom Perry Special Collections. Morrison also related his suspicion of presses in New Mexico and Oklahoma in this letter. He may have destroyed this material.

[373] Typed Letter Copy, William V. Morrison to Friend Leland [Sonnichsen], March 28, 1977, Sonnichsen Collection, University of Texas at El Paso, Special Collections, Box 136, Folder 1073.   This communication indicated that Sonnichsen and Morrison might have differences over contractual terms in their co-authored work.   Privately, Professor Sonnichsen distanced himself from Morrison's more controversial standings.

[374] William V. Morrison to Ms. Barbara Franklin, December 14, 1976, Sonnichsen Collection, University of Texas at El Paso, Special Collections, Box 136, Folder 1073.   From the later letter to Sonnichsen, the phrasing on the topic was nuanced. Morrison had plans on the issue some five years later, when he planned to bring up the subject yet again during the 100th anniversary of the outlaw's death.

[375] Obit, "Morrison,"[William V. Morrison], *El Paso Herald-Post,* August 31, 1977; K.F. Osthimer to Chaves County Historical Society, April 13, 1981, Billy the Kid Morgue File, Southeastern New Mexico Historical Society. Tunstill tended to be extreme in his publications, while Osthimer focused on the Santa Fe Ring. By the late 1980s, Tunstill moved and Osthimer passed away. Tunstill's publications are hard to find and considered rare books today.

[376] "Billy the Kid's Tombstone Stolen," *Springfield [MO] News-Leader,* February 5, 1981; Jim Bradshaw, "Tombstone of Billy the Kid Getting Free Ride Home," *Albuquerque Journal,* February 12, 1981.

[377] Obituary, Lois Telfer, *Bronx Press Review,* September 1, 1983.

[378] Phone Interview, Myrl Jane Humphrey, October 7, 2013; Entry, "John and Mary Jane Humphrey," Bob Parsons, ed., *Living Water: Our Mid-Pecos History : The Families & Events from Fort to Future* (Unknown: Mid-Pecos Historical Foundation, 1983), 131; John Humphrey, Beneficiary Identification Records

Locator Subsystem Death File, Department of Veterans Affairs, Record Group (RG) 15, National Archives and Records Administration, Tomas O. Martinez, "Museum Competes With Historical Trust, *Albuquerque Journal*, July 23, 1978; Matt Bosisio, "La Paloma Museum Preserves Past," *Roswell Daily Record*, July 28, 1985; "Lincoln Man established town museum," *El Paso Times*, September 25, 1989.

[379] "Famed N.M. Artist Peter Hurd Dies," *Albuquerque Journal*, July 10, 1984; "N.M. Painter Wyeth was Critic of TV, Feminism," *Albuquerque Journal,* April 4, 1997; Obituary, "Liggett Meigs," *Lubbock Avalanche-Journal*, September 6, 2003.

[380] Obituary, Louis A. Bowdre Sr., *Bartlesville Examiner-Enterprise*, December 31, 2004; "Bartlesville honors...Louis A. Bowdre," *Bartlesville Examiner-Enterprise*, July 16, 2002; Anthony DellaFlora, "State Not Kidding Around," *Albuquerque Journal,* June 11, 2003; Rene Romo, "Digging for the Truth," *Albuquerque Journal*, August 24, 2003; Interview Notes, Sue Tennell, September 9, 2013. Romo's article, which noted a request for DNA from Catherine Antrim, the mother of Billy the Kid, in Silver City, New Mexico, featured quotes from then-Fort Sumner Mayor Ray Lopez that opposed any dig in their cemetery. To the author's knowledge, no official effort was seriously considered for the same reason Judge Hensley ruled on in 1962. Rather, the Lincoln County Sheriff's Case was based on a comparison through DNA extracted from the Maxwell workbench. A subsequent ruling in Silver City to deny the extraction of DNA from the remains of Catherine Antrim, coupled with the recall of De Baca County Sheriff Gary Graves, effectively ended any real hope for this.

[381] Obituary, Lloyd Davis, *Albuquerque Journal*, March 9, 2016; Interview, Sharon Degner, July 18, 2013.

[382] With so many dispersions and flaws in the public record, the historical significance of the 1961-62 Telfer hearing is obvious. Instead of bringing the desired conclusion to the story of Billy the Kid, it left open questions. The mystery was left to solve without anyone seeing an identified body, no matter how correct and logical Judge Hensley's ruling was. It would have answered the "Brushy Bill" controversy at the very least.

BIBLIOGRAPHY

General Primary Sources

Abreu Family. Copy of Letter in Author's Possession.

Adams, Ramon Collection. Dallas Public Library. Dallas, Texas.

Bacon, Alfred T. Papers. Denver Public Library. Western History and Genealogy Department. Denver, Colorado.

Bacon Family Papers. Rhode Island Historical Society. Providence, Rhode Island.

Ball, Eve Papers. 20th Century Western and Mormon Manuscripts. L. Tom Perry Special Collections. Brigham Young University. Provo, Utah.

Blazer Family Papers. University of Arizona Special Collections. Tucson, Arizona.

Bonney, William H. Collection. Palace of the Governors, Fray Angelico Chavez History Library. Santa Fe, New Mexico.

Briscoe Center for American History. University of Texas Special Collections. Austin, Texas. Miscellaneous Collections.

Cline, Donald Collection of New Mexico Research Materials. 1959-032. State Archives of New Mexico. Santa Fe, New Mexico.

Cooke, Philip St. George III Collection. 1972-002. State Archives of New Mexico. Santa Fe, New Mexico.

De Baca County [NM] Courthouse. Records.

DeWitt County [MS]. Records.

Department of Veterans Affairs. Record Group 15. Beneficiary Identification Records Locator Subsystem Death File. National Archives & Records Administration.

Dykes, [Jeff] Collection. Cushing Memorial Library and Archives. Texas A&M University Special Collections. College Station, Texas.

Fulton, Maurice Garland Collection. University of Arizona Special Collections. Tucson, Arizona.

Historical Society for Southeast New Mexico. Roswell, New Mexico. Morgue File.

History Colorado Center. Hart Research Library. MSS 3079. Letter.

Keleher, William A. Papers. University of New Mexico, Center for Southwest Research. Albuquerque, New Mexico.

Lavash, Donald Papers. Copy in Author's Possession.

Lincoln County Collection. Palace of the Governors. Santa Fe, New Mexico.

Lincoln County [NM] Courthouse. Records.

Mississippi State Archives. Jackson, MS. Payne Family Subject File.

Mullin, Robert N. Collection. Haley Memorial Library & History Center. Midland, Texas.

Records of United States Army Commands. Record Group 393. National Archives & Records Administration.

Social Security Administration. Index and Master File. Record Group 47. National Archives & Records Administration.

Sonnichsen, C.L. Papers. MS141. University of Texas at El Paso, Special Collections.

Texas Department of State Health Services. Austin, Texas.

U.S. Army Enlistment Records, World War I. Record Group 64. National Archives & Records Administration.

United States Census, Population Schedules. Record Group 29. National Archives & Records Administration.

Vandale, Earl Collection. University of Texas at Austin. Dolph Briscoe Center for American History.

Works Progress Administration (WPA) Files. Library of Congress Manuscript Division.

Interviews

Davis, Lloyd. Ruidoso, New Mexico. April 29, 2014.

Degner, Sharon Sargent (and Eugene Degner). Alamogordo, New Mexico. July 18, 2013.

Humphrey, Myrl Jane. Phone, Dallas, Texas Area. October 7, 2013.

Jones, Nellie Ruth. Glencoe, New Mexico. October 16, 2013.

Salazar, Joe. Salazar Canyon, New Mexico. ca. October 2013.

Stearns, Johnson. Carrizozo, New Mexico. October 20, 2013.

Stewart, Harold and Mike. Eastland, Texas, January 10, 2009.

Tennell, Sue. Bartlesville, Oklahoma. September 9, 2013.

Letters, etc.

Ancestry.com. *Social Security Death Index, Master File.*

[Bonney, Cecil] to Jeff Dykes. March 1962. Postcard in Author's Collection.

Find-A-Grave. Database and Images.

Grabbe, Betty. Emails to Author.

Rosenblum, Enid to Author. May 15, 2015. Letter.

Scott, Phil. Mailed Information.

Books

Adams, Ramon F. *A Fitting Death for Billy the Kid.* Norman, OK: University of Oklahoma Press, 1960.

Anaya, A.F. (Paco). *I Buried Billy.* College Station, TX: Creative Publishing Company, 1991.

Bartholomew, Ed. *Jesse Evans-A Texas Hide-Burner.* Houston, TX: Frontier Press of Texas, 1955.

Blakestad, Alice, comp. *A Gravesite Directory of Cemeteries in Lincoln County.* Hondo, NM: Lincoln County Historical Society, 2001.

Bonney, Cecil. *Looking Over My Shoulder-Seventy-five Years in the Pecos Valley.* Roswell, NM: Hall-Poorbaugh Press, Inc., 1971.

Branch, Louis Leon. "Los Bilitos": "Billy the Kid" and His Gang. New York: Hearthstone Book [Carlton Press, Inc.], 1980.

Bryan, Howard. *Wildest of the Wild West-True Tales of a Frontier Town on the Santa Fe Trail.* Santa Fe, NM: Clear Light Publishers, 1988.

Burns, Walter Noble. *The Saga of Billy the Kid.* New York: Grosset & Dunlap Publishers, 1926.

Burroughs, Jeans M. *On the Trail-The Life and Tales of "Lead Steer" Potter.* Santa Fe, NM: Museum of New Mexico Press, 1980.

Burton, Clarence Monroe, William Stocking, and Gordon K. Miller, eds. *The City of Detroit, Michigan, 1701-1922, Volume 3.* Detroit and Chicago, IL: S.J. Clarke Publishing Co., 1922.

Caldwell, Clifford R. *John Simpson Chisum-The Cattle King of the Pecos Revisited.* Santa Fe, NM: 2010.

Coe, George W. [Doyce B. Nunis, Jr.] *Frontier Fighter-The autobiography of George W. Coe who fought and rode with Billy the Kid.* Chicago: R.R. Donnelley & Sons Company, 1984.

Coe, Wilbur. *Ranch on the Ruidoso-The Story of a Pioneer Family in New Mexico, 1871-1968.* New York: Alfred A. Knopf, 1969.

Dworkin, Mark J. *American Mythmaker-Walter Noble Burns and the Legends of Billy the Kid, Wyatt Earp, and Joaquin Murrieta.* Norman, OK: University of Oklahoma Press, 2015.

Dykes, J.C. *Billy the Kid-The Bibliography of a Legend.* Albuquerque, NM: University of New Mexico Press, 1952.

Dykes, Jeff C. *Law on a Wild Frontier.* Washington, D.C.: Potomac Corral of Westerners, May 1969.

Earle, James H. *The Capture of Billy the Kid.* College Station, TX: Creative Publishing Company, 1988.

Eastwood, Rich. *Nuestras Madres-A Story of Lincoln County New Mexico.* Author, ca. 2009.

Fleming, Elvis E. *Captain Joseph C. Lea-From Confederate Guerrilla to New Mexico Patriarch.* Las Cruces, NM: Yucca Tree Press, 2002.

Fuller, Mark S. *Never a Dull Moment-The Life of John Liggett Meigs.* Santa Fe, NM: Sunstone Press, 2015.

Fulton, Maurice G. *Roswell in its Early Years.* Roswell, NM: Hall-Poorbaugh Press, Inc., 1968.

Garrett, Patrick F. [Maurice G. Fulton, ed.] *Authentic Life of Billy the Kid.* New York: MacMillan Co., 1927.

Hertzog, Peter. *Little Known Facts about Billy, the Kid,* No. 3. Santa Fe, NM: Press of the Territorian, 1964.

Historical Reminiscences and Biographical Memoirs of Conway County, Arkansas. Little Rock, AR: Historical Publishing Company, 1890.

Hoyt, Henry F. *A Frontier Doctor.* Boston and New York: Houghton Mifflin Company, 1929.

Hutchinson, W.H. *A Bar Cross Man-The Life & Personal Writings of Eugene Manlove Rhodes.* Norman, OK: University of Oklahoma Press, 1956.

John Meigs: The Collectors Eye. Las Cruces, NM: University Art Gallery, New Mexico State University, 1997.

Johnson, Barry C., ed. *English Westerners' Brand Book, Vol. 5, No. 2.* 1963.

Keleher, William A. *Violence in Lincoln County 1869-1881-A New Mexico Item.* Albuquerque, NM: University of New Mexico Press, 1957.

Klasner, Lily [Eve Ball, ed.] *My Girlhood Among Outlaws.* Tucson, AZ: University of Arizona Press, 1972.

Lavash, Donald R. *Wilson and the Kid.* College Station, TX: Creative Publishing Company, 1990.

McAlavy, Don and Harold Kilmer. *High Plains History of East-Central New Mexico.* Clovis, NM: High Plains Historical Press, 1980.

McCarty, John L. *Maverick Town-The Story of Old Tascosa.* Norman, OK: University of Oklahoma Press, 1946.

Metz, Leon. *Pat Garrett-The Story of a Western Lawman.* Norman, OK: University of Oklahoma Press, 1974.

Miller, Nyle H. and Joseph W. Snell. *Great Gunfighters of the Kansas Cowtowns, 1867-1886.* Lincoln, NE: University of Nebraska Press, 1963.

Mullin. Robert N., ed. *Maurice Garland Fulton's History of the Lincoln County War.* Tucson, AZ: University of Arizona Press, 1968.

Nolan, Frederick W. *The Life & Death of John Henry Tunstall.* Albuquerque, NM: University of New Mexico Press, 1965.

O'Neil, James B. *They Die But Once-The Story of a Tejano.* New York: Knight Publications, Inc., 1935.

Otero, Miguel Antonio. *The Real Billy the Kid: with new light on the Lincoln County War, Facsimile of Original 1936 Edition.* Santa Fe, NM: Sunstone Press, 2007.

Parsons, Bob, ed. *Living Water: Our Mid-Pecos History: The Families & Events from Fort to Future.* Unknown: Mid-Pecos Historical Foundation, 1983.

Poe, John W. *The Death of Billy the Kid.* Boston and New York: Houghton Mifflin Company and Cambridge, MA: The Riverside Press, 1933.

Poe, Sophie A. *Buckboard Days.* Albuquerque, NM: University of New Mexico Press, 1981.

Potter, Col. Jack. *Cattle Trails of the Old West.* Clayton, NM: Laura R. Krehbiel, 1939.

Rasch, Philip J. [R.K. DeArment, ed.] *Gunsmoke in Lincoln County.* Stillwater, OK: Western Publications [National Association for Outlaw and Lawman History], 1997. In Affiliation with the University of Wyoming, Laramie, WY.

Rasch, Philip J. [R.K. DeArment, ed.] *Trailing Billy the Kid.* Stillwater, OK: Western Publications [National Association for Outlaw and Lawman History], 1995. In Affiliation with the University of Wyoming, Laramie, WY.

Rasch, Philip J. [R.K. DeArment, ed.] *Warriors of Lincoln County.* Stillwater, OK: Western Publications [National Association for

Outlaw and Lawman History], 1998. In Affiliation with the University of Wyoming, Laramie, WY.

Shinkle, James D. *Fort Sumner and the Bosque Redondo Indian Reservation.* Roswell, N.M.: Hall-Poorbaugh Press, Inc., 1965.

Sonnichsen, C.L. and William V. Morrison. *Alias Billy the Kid.* Barto, PA: Creative Texts Publishers, 2014.

Stanley, F. *Desperadoes of New Mexico.* Denver, CO: The World Press, Inc., 1953.

Stearns, Johnson S. and Ann Buffington. *Looking Back-A Photo History of Carrizozo-In Commemoration of Carrizozo's Centennial 1899-1999.* Carrizozo, NM: Lincoln County Historical Society, ca. 1999.

Stearns, Johnson S. *Small Town Magic.* White Oaks, NM: Birdsong's Press, 1997.

Stratton, Porter A. *The Territorial Press of New Mexico 1834-1912.* Albuquerque, NM: University of New Mexico Press, 1969.

Tunstill, William A. *Billy the Kid and Me Were the Same.* Roswell, NM: Western History Research Center, 1988.

Turk, David S. *Blackwater Draw.* Santa Fe, NM: Sunstone Press, 2011.

Wilson, John P., ed. *Pat Garrett and Billy the Kid as I Knew Them-Reminiscences of John P. Meadows.* Albuquerque, NM: University of New Mexico Press, 2004.

Magazine or Blog Articles

Anderson, Lillie Gerhardt. "Historic Fort Sumner." *New Mexico Magazine.* November 1952.

Douglas, Cameron. "Hello Bob." *True West Blog.* April 28, 2015.

Edwards, Harold L. "Barney Mason-In the Shadow of Pat Garrett and Billy the Kid." *Old West,* Summer 1990.

Gimlin, Hoyt. "Two New Mexico Towns Fight for the Remains of Billy the Kid." *Milwaukee Journal Green Sheet.* June 30, 1961.

Kelly, Bill. "Bowdre Mystery Yet to be Laid to Rest." *New Mexico Magazine.* February 1993.

Lavash, Donald. "Thomas G. Yerby and Nasaria." *The Outlaw Gazette,* December 1992.

McCright, Grady E. "Who Sleeps in Billy the Kid's Tomb?" *True Frontier*, April 1978.

McGaw, Kate. "The Faces of Lincoln Town." *New Mexico Magazine.* January 1983.

"Says Pete Maxwell-I Had Three Chances to be Killed." *Tinnie's Historical Roundup.* Volume III, No. 3, July 1981.

Smith, Debs. "The Battle for Billy's Bones." *Impact [Albuquerque Journal Magazine].* April 7, 1961.

Wilson, John P. "With His Boots Off: First Newspaper Reports on the Death of Billy the Kid." *Rio Grande History.* No. 14, 1983.

Newspapers

Alamogordo [Daily] News.

Albuquerque Citizen.

Albuquerque Journal.

Albuquerque Tribune.

Amarillo Globe.

Arizona Republic.

Austin American-Statesman.

Bartlesville [OK] Examiner-Enterprise.

Binghamton [NY] Press and Sun-Bulletin.

Bronx Press Review.

Buffalo Morning News and Illustrated Buffalo Express.

Burlington [Vermont] Free Press.

Clovis News-Journal.

De Baca County News.

Denver Times.

Deseret Evening News.

DeSoto Times.

Detroit Free Press.

El Paso Herald-Post.

El Paso Times.

Fairbanks [Alaska] Daily News-Miner.

Hartford Courant.

Hood County [TX] News.

Houston Chronicle.

Las Cruces Sun-News.

Las Vegas [Daily] Optic.

Lincoln County News [and Carrizozo Outlook].

Longview News-Journal.

Lubbock Avalanche-Journal.

[McAllen, Texas] Monitor.

Mesilla Independent.

New York Times.

[Provo, Utah] Daily Herald.

Quay County [NM] Sun.

Rocky Mountain News.

Roswell Daily Record.

Ruidoso News.

Santa Fe New Mexican.

Santa Fe Reporter.

Springfield News Leader.

Taos News.

Trinidad [CO] Chronicle News.

Tulsa World.

Watonga Herald.

ABOUT THE AUTHOR

David S. Turk is the Historian of the United States Marshals Service, and has served in this capacity since October 2001.

He is the author of six books and numerous articles on Many subjects related to investigative or Law Enforcement history. Of note is *Forging The Star,* which untangles the complicated history of the U.S. Marshals Service in its modern era. Another is *Blackwater Draw*, a focused study on the Murders of three enemies of Billy the Kid in Lincoln County, New Mexico Territory.

His interest in investigative history progressed from cases studies within his work, including Billy the Kid and the Lincoln County War. The latter began as an agency study, and progressed into a personal passion.

He was raised in Virginia, graduated from George Mason University, and served as Past President of their History Alumni. for several years, he was Treasurer in the Society for History in the Federal Government.

THANK YOU FOR READING!

If you enjoyed this book, we would appreciate your customer review on your book seller's website or on Goodreads.

Also, we would like for you to know that you can find more great books like this one at www.CreativeTexts.com

www.ingramcontent.com/pod-product-compliance
Lightning Source LLC
Chambersburg PA
CBHW031938090426
42811CB00002B/228